HEARTBROKEN
Open

A True Story
of Coming Alive Again
After Profound Loss

KRISTINE CARLSON

Advance praise for HEARTBROKEN OPEN

"Unanticipated death renders those left behind with feelings of rawness combined with shock and disbelief. Kristine Carlson's ability to describe the poignant moments on her journey to gain the hope required to begin healing and her determination to continue the legacy that she and her husband Richard created together is inspirational. *Heartbroken Open* is a resource of profound lessons that sometimes can only be found in the depths of despair, including overcoming fear and sharing her teachings for returning to a happy, contented life. I recommend this read not only for all widows but for widow supporters searching to better understand what widows encounter and endure."

Carolyn Caple Moor, Developmental Director, Modern Day Widow's Club

"Kristine Carlson welcomes readers into her heartbreak after the death of her husband, Dr. Richard Carlson, with an honesty and vulnerability that takes your breath away. But she doesn't leave us breathless; she walks us through her awakening to the power of gratitude and teaches us that broken hearts have an increased capacity for love. Richard Carlson inspired millions of people through his life-affirming work. His sudden death altered Kristine's world and required her to explore both her pain and her potential as she built a new life of purpose. This book will provide you with the tools to do the same, no matter what challenge you face."

Michele Neff Hernandez, Founder of Soaring Spirits International, author of *Different After You: Rediscovering Yourself and Healing after Grief or Trauma*, and a 2021 CNN Hero

"With a soul that is a brilliant light force and a voice that reads like a fiction novel you can't put down, Kristine Carlson shakes the ground that grief has laid for us all with this book that will forever stay in your life's journey. Her love for Richard is loud and penetrating. Her life after losing him changed forever. But what always remains is that light force that you will take with you when this book is read and explored. Unforgettable and untamable – just like life after devastating loss."

Christina Rasmussen, author of *Second Firsts*, Founder of Life Starters

"Richard Carlson's death affected many of us, but none more powerfully or painfully than his wife and children. Kristine Carlson has gloriously owned her own voice since Richard's death, and now gives words and meaning to her extraordinary journey through grief to healing. She shines even more beautifully for having allowed such pain to penetrate her heart and to ultimately teach her what it means to be alive. This book is a healing balm for the broken heart."

Marianne Williamson, author of *A Return of Love*

"Kristine Carlson has created a wonderfully rich, deeply engaging, heartfelt journey through the peaks and valleys of profound loss. This book is a bountiful gift … riveting, intensely moving, and, most of all, enormously instructive and helpful."

John Welshons, author of *One Soul, One Love, One Heart*

"Kristine Carlson shares her story of grief and transformation with raw honesty, eloquence, and humanness. It will open your heart to the true spirit of love. I couldn't put it down till I savored each page."

Joseph Baily, co-author of *Slowing Down to the Speed of Life*

"Kristine Carlson's courageous story about loss, grief, and the immeasurable strength of love is deeply inspiring and empowering."

Marci Shimoff, author of *Happy For No Reason* and *Chicken Soup for the Soul*

"In times of crisis and chaos that cause many to crumble, heroes emerge. Kristine Carlson is one such person. *Heartbroken Open* is brilliant! Kristine Carlson gives you the keys to powerful living. This book is a gift for the loving and healing heart."

Dr. Pat Baccili, *The Dr. Pat Show*

"This is a beautiful book – clear and strong, as is its author, who details so poignantly her navigation through the rough, murky, and ultimately healing waters of grief. *Heartbroken Open* is a memoir, but also a guide through loss to redemption and reinvention."

Victoria Moran, author of *Creating a Charmed Life*

"At last a book that dares to face grief head-on. Heartbroken Open is an unswerving, heart-wrenching, unexpectedly sublime memoir about having loved and lost. Kristine's candid yet gentle narrative escorts you through and beyond the more familiar territory of the psyche and plummets straight into the astonishing healing wisdom of the soul. If you have ever been in love, and wonder how you would survive without it, you absolutely must read this book!"

Maryanne Comaroto, relationship expert and author of *Hindsight*

ALSO BY KRISTINE CARLSON

Don't Sweat the Small Stuff for Women: *Simple and Practical Ways to Do What Matters Most and Find Time for You*

Don't Sweat the Small Stuff for Moms: *Simple Ways to Stress Less and Enjoy Your Family More*

From Heartbreak to Wholeness: *The Hero's Journey to Joy*

The What Now? Course *and Workbook*

21 days of Grieving with Grace *With Kristine Carlson*

BOOKS BY RICHARD AND KRISTINE CARLSON

An Hour to Live, an Hour to Love: *The Story of the Best Gift Ever Given*

Don't Sweat the Small Stuff in Love: *Simple Ways to Nurture and Strengthen Your Relationship While Avoiding the Habits That Break Down Your Loving Connection*

Happiness Training Courses:
Visit **dontsweat.com**

Visit Kristine Carlson at **kristinecarlson.com**

HEARTBROKEN
Open

A True Story
of Coming Alive Again
After Profound Loss

KRISTINE CARLSON

BOOK DOULAS PUBLISHING

Kristine Carlson
Heartbroken Open
Book Doulas Publishing
Copyright © 2011, 2021 by Kristine Carlson
Second Edition

The previous edition of this work was published by
HarperOne, San Francisco, California in 2011.

Print ISBN: 978-1-7378563-0-6
Ebook (Kindle) ISBN: 978-1-7378563-1-3

Book Design | Petya Tsankova
Editor | Susan Leon
Author Portrait Photography | Alyssa Martens

Publishing Support | TSPA The Self Publishing Agency, Inc.

This book is dedicated in loving memory of

Richard Carlson

*who has been my greatest teacher
and whose love moved me in life and through
the corridor of loss.*

And, to our first grandson

*Caden Richard
born August 10, 2009.*

*Dear sweet Grandson, you are the joy-filled
beginning in this ending as the cycle of life
carries on.*

*And to all of our grandkids
Kayson, Kennedy, Cambree and Cannon—you are all a legacy of love.*

CONTENTS

ACKNOWLEDGEMENTS

First, I want to acknowledge my daughters, Jasmine Priddy and Kenna Carlson. They have been my greatest support and encouragement. Courageous in their own grief, they have both shown up with resiliency and strength for me and for each other. My daughters have created beautiful lives, and their father would be as proud of them as I am. It has been a messy journey, but as a family, we've traversed the path of healing together.

My parents, Pat and Ted Anderson, have always cheered me on and have taught me so much about how to live a good life of hope and faith in God.

Special thanks to all of my good friends and family – all who have held me dear in a safety net of love.

I'm so grateful to Maura Dunbar and Mark Teitelbaum for their unwavering tenacity in making this story into a Lifetime movie, and to Heather Locklear for taking on the role of a woman in grief to bring my story to life.

Thanks to my Book Doulas business partner, Debra Evans, for her unwavering support.

Thank you to all the folks at The Self Publishing Agency for birthing this new edition.

PROLOGUE

THE MUSLIDE: LIFE PREPARES US

We can only connect the dots by looking back on life.
Steve Jobs, 2005 Stanford Commencement

December 30, 2005, one year before my husband died

The day was blustery and held the promise of a turbulent storm. I tossed and turned during the night as the rain pelted the windows. Our oak trees, over a hundred years old, protested and crackled as they stretched to the ground like yogis stretching into downward dog. I snuggled into Richard and said aloud, "Hon, this can't be good."

These kinds of storms wreak havoc on California clay. The sandy soil dries up in drought every year, and if not for the sprinklers, the land would be destined for desert. The hillsides are thirsty and saturate quickly for lack of drainage. As the underground springs rise to the surface, they carve and fill every crevice, making a new path for movement and flooding.

I had never heard water roar off the house like this before. As the storm raged and the wind howled and dawn approached, I remarked, laughed even, about how lucky we were to live on *top* of the hill (no flooding for *us*). Of course, now I know that each home has a way of teaching you more about real estate through experience. And, if you live in a place long enough, you'll know all its inner workings because you've had to either fix it, or completely rebuild it, piece by piece. Little did I know that our beautiful Craftsman style house, our home for only two years, was about to give us an education in hillside drainage.

All the water from our home, we would discover, was dispelled at the top instead of being taken to the bottom of the slope as specified by its building engineer. As a result, we would learn the hard way that even expensive homes follow their own law, and that there are no safeguards from natural disaster.

The storm ceased for a brief reprieve. We decided to grab some Starbucks and check on our horses, stabled about a mile away. Descending the hill, we saw tree branches and limbs scattered like skeleton bones across the community. As we rounded the bend en route to the bottom, nothing looked right. We stopped short. The road had disappeared under several feet of heavy brown mud. I looked to my right. A craggy hole was all that remained where the earth had let go of itself and slid itself into a mound on the construction of a new home some twenty feet on the other side. Suddenly it registered. "Oh, God. It's a mudslide! Oh, Gooooooood! It's our mudslide," I moaned.

Then suddenly, alert to that reality, we simultaneously panic-whispered, "Shit!" At 7:00 A.M., on the cusp of New Year's Eve, the only road to our gated community was impassable. As we opened our car doors and stepped out to assess the damage, I saw fierceness in my husband's gaze, a determination in the furl of his brow, as he started to calculate the task in front of him.

We backed our SUV up to the house. As he retrieved the shovel from our garage, I begged him not to remove the dirt himself. My anger rising, I said, "Richard, your back won't take this."

Richard suffered chronic back pain due to the excessive effort he had spent in his youth achieving a 135-mile-per-hour serve and with it, a top national tennis ranking during college. But something had shifted; for the past two years, he endured lower lumbar agony while resisting pain medication and attempting to live life normally. I had to do all that I could to stand in the way of Richard further disabling himself.

At times the spasms were so bad he would just lie in bed on his side with a pillow between his legs, breathing, gazing blankly, yet peacefully. I once asked him what it felt like and he said, "If your fingers were stuck in a doorjamb and the door was closed *and* you had an elephant standing on the small of your back, on a scale of one-to-ten it would be ten plus; *that's* what it feels like." He suffered this way, nerve on nerve, sometimes for days. There were many times he was bent at a 45-degree angle when he got out of the car to run a simple errand. There were days I could barely recognize the erect stature of the 6-foot-3½ inch man I married.

We sought medical options, but surgeons were reluctant to commit to the complex series of disk replacements we felt would give him his best chance; they were uncertain that surgery would help. It could even cripple him. He tried every alternative: physical therapy, acupuncture, biofeedback, vitamins, swimming. You name it, he tried it. But Richard was characteristically graceful in how he managed his pain. He rarely complained, and only when asked would he admit to his discomfort.

Much of our pastime as a couple was spent running, often training for marathons. He used to say life wouldn't be the same if he couldn't exercise. Even when he reached the point where he couldn't exercise by pushing the outer limits of physical endurance, he remained present and even peaceful. His spine was literally disintegrating. He suffered greatly, and my personal pain was the impotence I felt watching him.

But at this moment, there was no stopping him. He spoke with dead calm, "The road is closed and there are neighbors who are elderly. Someone might have a heart attack. It has to be done. I need to clear this road immediately."

As reports on the radio indicated, this was one of the worst Bay Area storms in years, and there were mudslides everywhere. There was little promise of getting a tractor to our house anytime soon. After shoveling unwaveringly for four hours, Richard collapsed, and so did his spine.

Crisis hits and you respond. All the while you think you are making "level-headed" decisions and creating a plan. All the while you are responding to something bigger than you even know.

The only neighbors who could have helped us were tending to their own mudslide. By this time the following year, they would be in full divorce proceedings and Richard would be gone.

Richard rested and I drove to the nearest hardware store, where I was directed to a mound of sand as well as bags, ties, and shovels. I joined the other men and their silence at the mound. I felt strange, like I was in a dream. I had never filled a sandbag in my princess life (though I *had* mucked many stalls). I mimicked the men until methodically and rhythmically, I had filled and loaded fifty 35-pound bags in the back of my SUV. Unaccustomed to manual labor, my arms felt like rubber hands.

I was oddly fascinated by the moment – exhilarated to be the only woman there. I am strong for my size, as athletic fitness has always been a priority. We were an odd-looking bunch. All of us appeared as though we had just rolled out of bed, our movements synchronized by a community in crisis. I offered the only comment any one of us made, "Well, this is a hell of a way to start the New Year!" No one laughed. Looking back, I think that was out of a simple need to conserve energy, an indication that this was just the beginning of a very long day.

I brought the sandbags home, and bless Richard's heart, he dragged his aching back up and down that hill for a few more hours. We sandbagged and blue-tarped the lower part of the hill, filling a crater swollen to a size of 14 by 12 feet, working our way up the hole, side by side. With the mud clumping to the bottom of our shoes, it was like wearing leg weights while climbing a soft sand hill carrying 35 pounds up a flight of steep stairs. It was the kind of climb that could leave your legs tired after the first try. We did this at least fifty times.

We stood at the bottom of the hole. We held hands, gripping each other in teamwork, sunk to our ankles in mud. Richard looked at me with a mixture of sadness and stress, the kind that comes from discomfort, exhaustion, and the sort of pain that is so deep its end is also its beginning. The only time I had ever seen him in such physical duress was when he collapsed from paralyzing leg cramps during a marathon, just a hundred feet from the finish line. His fellow runners lifted and pushed him as he willed himself to a sprint to break three hours.

Now, with tears in his eyes, he looked at me intently and said, "I'm so sorry, Kris, I can't help you finish this." I was on my own.

I searched the house for supplies as Richard lay down, more tortured by his feeling of impotence than by his wracking back spasms. Unable to find rope or string, I settled upon shoelaces. I put a straw into my pocket because I wasn't sure how stable the earth was as it loomed over my head. I knew what skiers in avalanche country were told to do. It was just one of many moments of lucidity that day.

Eventually, I intuited the most effective way to drive, toss, and then maneuver the many sandbags to their respective places. Alone, I did this over and over, careful with each step in and out of the depth of the earth, into and out of an abyss of nature. By four o'clock I had been working without food and rest since daybreak.

I bent like a broken beanstalk in tears of surrender. I sobbed uncontrollably until I laughed out loud thinking of our friends, the masochists we called triathletes, marathoners, centurion cyclists, and rock climbers. They would have helped us happily, thinking this day was a great workout. It had all the elements of a true test of endurance: weight lifting, climbing hillsides, and it lasted for hours! I almost gave up. I heard my own voice say, "You are not a quitter! You are tough! You need to protect your home."

What kept us from calling for help? It was simple: We didn't want to inconvenience anyone over the New Year's holiday. We had no idea how big a problem we faced, at least not until the rain stopped and the sun revealed the damage. It would take 240,000 tons of rock and $60,000 of excavation to make that hill whole again.

For weeks we were immersed in recovery and the manic search for solutions – a solution to the hillside hole, and a solution to Richard's back agony. I wondered if all this confusion and instability was a manifestation of our personal universe from the inside out. I paused to ask, "In what way are we not on solid ground?"

Eleven months later I would have my answer.

One

SURRENDER

… To Grief and the Process of Healing

1.

SHATTERED

December 13, 2006

My life changed with a phone call.

I pulled into the parking space as my cell rang and I viewed a 718 area code. It was 12:40 P.M. on the Pacific Coast. I smiled with relief, thinking Richard was calling from New York to let me know his plane had landed and he was safe. He was probably already at the hotel - another business trip. We had our routine. I picked up the call, expecting to hear his familiar voice on the other end. Instead, a man and a woman spoke to me at once, their voices urgent and loud, as they began to fire questions at me with pronounced South Asian accents.

"Are you related to Richard Carlson?" they asked.

I replied pertly, "Who wants to know?" Richard was well known, a celebrity author, and over the years we had had our share of overeager fans. We had learned to be cautious, protective.

The man announced, "This is Jamaica Memorial Hospital in Queens, New York, calling.... Are you on a cell phone?"

I answered, "Yes, I am Richard's wife." Then they asked me if my car was parked. I shifted the phone to my other ear and pulled down the visor, squinting against the California sunlight. "Yes," I said again. "I am parked."

They said, "We have Mr. Carlson with us here at the hospital."

I began to panic. What could have happened on his transcontinental flight? Was he ill? I fired back, "Is he all right?" What the hell was happening? I was now feeling desperate to speak to him and was already thinking of how I could get to New York as quickly as possible.

They said, "No. We are sorry to inform you, Mrs. Carlson, that Mr. Carlson has expired."

There was an intense heat all around my head, like my head was in an oven. I felt I was going to throw up. I had heard about such things but never got it – the body's visceral response to news it cannot digest, like a response to food poisoning. I clawed the air, not grasping what I had just heard. I began to get angry, thinking this was a hell of a prank call. I screamed, "What? What! Expired! *Expired!* What the hell kind of word is *expired*, anyway?"

Then it became clear what these voices, these strangers without faces or compassionate eyes, were telling me. I knew what they meant, although I couldn't believe this was real. I kept asking, desperate for them to tell me that they were just kidding, that this was not happening. Over and over I repeated, "How do I know this is real?"

Then they described Richard's flight, and I *knew*. They said he had declined food, as he often did on flights because he wanted to work and rest. They said he was asleep when he died. They said he had heart failure, but they were unsure of the actual cause of death. The coroner later told me it had been a pulmonary embolism: a blood clot released from his leg traveling to his lung during the descent of the flight – lethal. It had been mercifully quick and painless. Nothing could have been done to save him.

Solemnly, I asked, "When?"

"About an hour and a half ago," they told me. And all I could think was, Oh my God. Just like that. There is nothing I can do to change this. He's *gone.* I began to make noises I had never made in my life, like an animal suffering. Like the screams I had heard beyond our window late one night when some small animal was about to be slaughtered by a coyote. This cry was coming from somewhere deep inside me as I died, too, with my true love that day.

I had to get out of the car to move my body; the car was too small for me because I was completely out of my head. I was crazy for several

4

minutes, perhaps ten minutes, or it could have been two. I don't really know how long I screamed but my throat felt scorched. Tears ran out of my eyes and burned dry. As I was screaming, I saw a woman who was passing by grab her little girl closely as if protecting her from some lunatic. I was pleading with God, realizing that there was no negotiation or wiggle room in this. I couldn't make any bargain or promise that would bring Richard back; it was too late. I felt helpless and hopeless as if I was crashing and spinning out of control, and completely alone. I couldn't breathe, and I willed my heart to stop beating. I screamed in a high pitch, "No, please. No! No! No! *No!*" I was still holding the phone as the voices on the other end began to fade. I threw my phone into the car.

Getting back into the car, I grabbed the steering wheel, hugging it tight. If there had been a burning fire, I would have thrown myself on top of it. Then there was a thought, a question that interrupted. "What is your worst nightmare?" It penetrated and pierced me like an arrow, a flash of a conversation I had with Richard. We talked about this and had agreed. We had said that losing our daughters would be more difficult than losing each other.

Suddenly I could see my girls' faces as I squeezed my eyes closed – Jasmine and Kenna. They were seventeen and fourteen. Their lives were before them, lives that would stop, too, like mine just had. I continued to hold the steering wheel, my knuckles turning white, as if I were in a hurricane and it was the only way to stay grounded. In that instant, a vision of my daughters came to me and, like a vacuum of energy, I felt myself return to my body. I knew the one thing that would be worse than this would be a phone call telling me that something had happened to them. I heard Richard's voice, whispering as in the lunar curve of a dream, "Kris, they need you more than ever now. You are meant to stay." I have never felt such heaviness in my heart or dread in my soul as I realized life would be forever different now. I had never imagined a life without Richard.

Survival impresses itself upon us. Even when we think we don't want to live, God presents a path that bridges us to the next moment. A friend sent me a bereavement card and in her own beautiful script wrote: "Think of what you would die for and live for that." Surely, that is what happened in a moment when I would have willed myself to die. The love that I had for our daughters saved my own life. I would die for them in a heartbeat, as I knew I would have died for Richard, and he for us.

2.

THE FIRST DAYS

Like a meteor suddenly hitting the earth, Richard's death blew our lives wide open.

I picked up my cell phone and tried to remember my girlfriends' numbers, numbers I called every day, but my mind went blank. I scrolled back through my call list and found the number of Laura, one of my best friends. Unfortunately, she did not pick up. Next, I tried Cindy, Richard's dear friend since childhood. She lived nearby. But it was as dangerous for her to drive as it was for me. When she got to me at the Sun Valley Mall, her upset was palpable. And Laura arrived, too, my message reaching her ten or fifteen minutes later.

"Kris," Laura said, "Do you have a number that I can call to verify this?" I handed her my phone. Looking at my caller ID, she dialed the 718 number. Speaking with the doctor and nurse I'd hung up on just a little while before, she bowed her head, drew in her breath, and nodded, her hand pressed against her mouth. Yes, it was true, all of it.

With this knowledge, I understood what I had to do. Richard and I were so close; living and working together enmeshed our lives in special ways. It was a beautiful, peaceful union; we didn't have the angst and edges that many couples have with one another. So, I knew I had to deal with this myself from the start. This had happened. It was real, and I had to be the one to tell those who had been closest to him. I had to make the phone calls myself.

But first there were his parents and then there were my girls. I called his father, Don. I can't remember the words I had chosen but it was an awful call. Richard was his parents' sunshine, and I didn't know how they would survive this news.

Laura drove me to our elder daughter's school. I had called Jazz to say that I was coming over, my broken voice giving me away. "What's wrong with Dad?" she demanded over the phone. When she heard me cry, something I never did, she knew. She began to sob, I told her I was on my way and made sure she was with someone who could hold her until I got there. As I drove up, she was sitting with a small group of supporters on the curb of the street. She sprang up and into my arms with only one question: "Why did this happen to Dad?" Next, we went to tell Kenna. She had just boarded a school bus on her way to a soccer game. She was smiling as she spotted me and came bouncing off the bus. Then she saw all of us, and she knew something was terribly wrong. As I told her, she fell to the ground, face to the earth, spread-eagled, crying hysterically, in front of a busload of kids.

We all went home together, disoriented, sobbing. I said something to the girls to try to make sense of this moment, but there wasn't any sense or order in any of it. As Laura pulled into my driveway I looked around and asked, "Why are there cars parked everywhere?"

Laura responded, "Your friends are here, honey. News like this travels fast."

My parents jumped on a plane immediately after I called. Melanie flew in from Utah, Lisa from Southern California. Mitch, one of Richard's best friends, came, as did the girls' closest friends. The house filled up fast. Instinctively, we tunneled to one another in our numbed amazement, staying close through the dangerous time of mitigating despair.

The worst minutes of those next hours were arranging for the organs of Richard's young and healthy body to be successfully harvested. I had to act fast, with clarity and with decisiveness. The decision to go ahead meant we would not see Richard again, even in death. But the girls wanted to remember him as he had lived, and without hesitation they also knew what their father's wishes would be. As a writer and a teacher, Richard gave people many gifts; from his private tragedy, we knew he would have wanted to give others the gift of life.

And yet, what had to be done was difficult to reconcile with what had not been processed. I began to sob, begging the woman tasked with coordinating the farming of his organs to go faster. She had so many questions needing immediate answers, and said there was no time to consult Richard's medical records. I pleaded that she hurry. My children were on the other side of the door, in distress. They needed me. And each question only reminded me that just hours before, my husband had been a living, breathing man. Thankfully, Laura stood behind me the entire time as I responded, often with her hand simply placed on my back or shoulder. That gesture alone strengthened me to finish the call.

When it was over, I was spent. I opened the door and walked into my daughters' arms. I held them without words. I didn't tell them that this was going to be okay. I didn't feel like it would ever be okay again. Still, eleven families would receive the best news of their lives from Richard's gifts on the worst day of ours. Staring blankly, I could only think of the person who would be lucky enough to see the world through Richard Carlson's eyes.

There is something inherently unfair when death comes unexpectedly. The disorder surrounding Richard's passing – no time to feel the brush of his fingertips on mine, no hushed intimacies or farewells – rocked me throughout those first twenty-four hours.

It was more than shock or sorrow. I felt an indescribable, unsettling disturbance, beyond the tree line, and past reason. Lights flickered on and off in our home. My body shook, vibrated actually, without stop from a place deep within. I received calls from friends all over the country, telling me that Richard was waking them up, confused about where he was, and I knew why I shook.

Our lives had been blessed with mystical experiences from our earliest days together. We looked to the universe to show us through "signs" that all was in order and we were on the right path. Coincidence, synchronicity, and listening for the manifestation of spiritual phenomena were not new to us. My life with Richard was filled with more than the average experience of mysticism. We saw those moments as part of the intentionality and the magic of life. And, yes, it was an abiding part of our daily life to notice and discuss these happenings. We looked for signs of the divine.

Richard, in fact, had many psychic dreams. "I think I accidentally time-traveled," he would say. He once dreamed weeks in advance that a filly named Winning Colors would win the Kentucky Derby title – by eight lengths. We went to the racetrack that Saturday, placed a bet, and won $1,500, which really helped because at the time we were completely broke. (And, by the way, the horse did win by eight lengths.) Richard had a deep intuition about the stock market crash in October of 1987, and he pulled our money out three days before the crash. Most amazing, he dreamed that his book, *Don't Sweat the Small Stuff*, would sell 3.2 million copies during its first year, and it did.

That night, as I restlessly tried to sleep, I remembered another dream he had told me about, a powerful premonition, seven years prior to his death. Richard, who traveled regularly, started having severe flight anxiety, so I asked him why. He said, "I had a very vivid dream that I died on an airplane."

"Did the plane have an accident in your dream?" I asked him.

"No," he told me. "Something happened to me. All I know is that I died. It seemed very real to me, and I've been frightened ever since."

Now in the darkness of my first night without him, I understood that between the lights, vibrations, and dreams many of his closest friends and I were experiencing, Richard had pierced an opening for us between our worlds, between our dimensions, as the news of his passing cracked us all open like eggs. This is known in some spiritual circles as "the veil thinning."

Often people who have known great loss will tell you they dream of their loved ones, and that those dreams are as real to them as a glass of milk sitting on the kitchen counter. I would dream very little about Richard during the first year, but over the next few months I was suddenly intensely sensitive to light, sound, and energy. I watched for signs of him everywhere: in the slanting afternoon light, in the mist that often rolls across our northern California sky, in the way I shivered with a sudden breeze. There were many conscious moments when I experienced him, too, and it seemed I felt him and noticed him in obvious ways every day. But now, with Richard's passing so fresh and raw, it was my deepest desire to open myself so that I could be wherever he was, so that I could feel his presence however fleetingly, and I knew he would show me signs.

For the first twenty-four hours after he died, I felt his confusion. And so, when my friend Yvonne called around ten o'clock in the evening of the second night without Richard to say she and her daughters were bringing over a friend, a young woman named Berenice who, she said, had a very special psychic gift, I was grateful. "Kris," Yvonne continued, "Berenice says Richard wants to speak with you. You can trust her. She sees the light and hears the voices of spiritual beings that have recently passed. There are things Richard has to say to you."

It seemed to me that yes, of course, because he had died so suddenly, Richard would find a way to say good-bye. I knew that love was always present, so I was open and ready for this.

A small group of us gathered on my bed and on the floor, and closed the door. As Berenice walked in, she drew an audible breath and raised her arms high. "What huge light!" she said. "I believe your husband's body could no longer house this powerful spirit."

I felt his soul longing to communicate. And so, in the course of our brief time together, she became the conduit of special messages for Jasmine, for Kenna, and for me. To Kenna, who worries so much about things, Berenice said, "Your father says you won't be able to worry your way out of this," but that his light would always be by her side, even when she experienced whatever lows were to come. To Jazz, our older daughter and a natural caretaker, he said that he wanted her to take care of herself first, and to know that her sister and I would be fine, that my reserves of strength and independence were deeper than I knew.

"He is holding you now," Berenice said to me. I felt embraced by warmth and energy as Richard's love surged through me and filled me; I felt like a candle being lit from within.

We had always loved on two planes, him and me, with one foot in the world of everyday and with the other in spirit, in dreams and the ephemeral. It's a beautiful place in which to live, but, in many ways, it's a challenging place, a place where the vibrations of the mystical are felt intensely, and where, through our daily ritual of meditation and prayer, we sought and received clues from the universe about our direction.

So, in this divine instant, with my girls beside me, my closest friends around me, the bedroom lighting low, a feeling of peace settled and a connection ran through me. I knew that Richard would not be lost to me forever. In the months ahead I would listen, with patience and wisdom, to understand why God had called him, why He had taken him from me and my girls. But right then, not being able to feel him, not knowing where he was, had been the worst feeling. It was important for me to know that he had crossed safely – like receiving the phone call after a long flight he never made that fateful day. Once he knew where he was, he had to communicate with us or else he wasn't going to move forward in this next journey. Our journey – my girls' and mine – was uncharted. But now I could feel his well-being. I knew that I would feel him again, always on love's light wings. I knew he had found his way. And with that, the energy in our home shifted, and the veil between us quietly vanished.

That other-worldly hour lifted us and carried us through the public events ahead. The following days were surreal. Everybody we had ever loved now rallied around us. Our immediate family and friends stayed close. I could feel the vibrating pulse of prayer from throughout the world as news of Richard's death spread and hundreds of thousands of people hit our website. Strangers posted memorial signs on their lawns. Internet messages numbering in the thousands appeared. Richard's wish, articulated casually long before, had been to be cremated. Our "private" memorial service of two hundred invitees swelled to seven hundred people, there to celebrate the life of Richard Carlson. I had underestimated all the communities we had been involved in, all the families and colleagues that our lives had touched and who had felt his impact.

The memorial service was planned in fifteen minutes. I woke the morning after the evening of the thinning veil and felt Richard once again guiding me, telling me what he would want. As people entered, Bobby McFerrin played "Don't Worry. Be Happy." I knew who Richard would want to speak about him. I also knew that he would hold me, steadying me like a cradle on the sea, as I did the unthinkable, taking the podium and speaking about him as his wife, soul mate and life partner. The girls found their courage, too, and joined me. Our arms wrapped around each other as the hundreds assembled there contemplated and honored him in celebration of his life. Love was everywhere. Everyone held hands as John Astin closed the service by singing one of Richard's favorite songs, "Love, Serve, and Remember."

The immediate crush of those days left me feeling exhausted but blessed. The day after the memorial, his beloved best friend, Ben, and I sat holding hands on his office floor talking about Richard. Then I looked up to a corner on the wall and asked, "Ben, what's that?" As bright as a flashlight in a dark room, there was a form with rhythmic pulsing in its center.

Ben said, "Oh my God, that's a human heart." We continued to hold hands and sat still for about thirty seconds as though watching a magician finish a trick. The light slowly shrank from the outer edges and then it was swiftly grabbed from the wall. We laughed as Ben joked that Richard was having some fun with us, and reminding us that his love was with us. Now that the profound shock to those who loved him and the solemnity of the memorial service had passed, it was time to begin to heal and move forward.

Just how I would do so would surprise me. Deep grief follows its own instruction.

3.

EMBRACING GRIEF

It was morning and the girls were getting ready for school for the first time since winter break. This was also their first day back since Richard had died almost three weeks before. I absentmindedly opened the trunk of my car. Until a few days ago our home had been busy with people coming and going, but now the restoration of old routines held the promise of comfort. It was our first attempt at moving through shock to settle back into life. We still felt like Richard was away on business and that any day he would return.

I pulled a fifty-pound bag of salt from the car. I would need to empty the bag manually into the water softener, a task Richard had always performed. I rested the bag against my thigh to check the weight to make sure I could carry it. I realized I could lift it and cradled it like a baby in my arms. Halfway to the water softener I was stopped by an invisible slap. I looked up at the sky breaking into daylight with hues of orange and purple mingling with winter clouds. I fell to my knees in what I would later recognize as my first true wave of despair.

I sobbed hard for several minutes, allowing myself to indulge in the unexpected contractions, leaning into them with odd satisfaction as my body expressed the inexpressible. I took full advantage of the privacy that the strange timing of this moment allowed. I didn't want to upset the girls before they left for school. So, after a few minutes, I took a deep breath, and then several more. I felt hopeless yet determined to complete this task. I opened the bag of salt. Lift. Pour. I felt the relief of the weight now weightless. I held the empty bag. The weight of our life, all of it, now belonged to me. I would carry on this journey … alone. Everything that was on Richard's list was now on mine.

Richard left and Grief moved in. Ingenious, resourceful, fluid, always in charge, grief became my constant companion and finally – my friend. Grief has a way of thrusting you into the present. Over the next few months I realized that I would have to surrender to this new life and allow grief to lead me to healing. Grief would take me inward across boundaries I had never gone in myself, into places I feared the most. The biggest initial hurdle, I came to understand, was surrender. I did not understand it at first, but surrender would be my access to healing – surrender to the permanent, unchangeable fact of my loss; surrender to the end of our sweet life; surrender to what *is,* not to what was or might have been. There would be no controlling life any longer, I would learn. This time, life required something more of me, a long, slow, pivot toward a new strategy for survival. Surrender was both a process and a path. My choice was only to take it, or to resist. The path of what is, *right now*, would allow the pain to spill out as my tears emptied me to liberation. I took it.

Many things changed to make room for grief in my house. Priorities shifted. Old beliefs died. My laundry room was a mess. I threw my clothes on the floor. I often saved dinner dishes for the morning because it made more sense to do them just once a day. In many ways, grief simplified our lives, taking us to the bare essentials.

The early days and weeks passed slowly. Each moment, like an hourglass emptying grains of sand from one side to the other, seemed to elongate endlessly. The girls and I couldn't eat or sleep. We moved a twin mattress from our guest room onto the floor next to my bed so Jazz and Kenna could alternate, one in bed with me and one on the mattress by the bed each night. I worried about them but, frozen in the fragility of the moment, I was barely functioning myself. Eventually, the girls returned to their rooms, and I slept alone.

I was used to sleeping alone sometimes, as Richard was often gone three or four days at a time, but this was different. When you're going through loss, sleep is disturbed. Getting into our bed each night made my loss feel closer and crueler. Sleeping alone reminded me that now I *was* alone. I would wake up a lot for long periods and then go back to sleep. I would watch the changing sky from our big bedroom window. Being in bed is such a lovely time when you've been mated. To have someone missing from your bed is disorienting; even the sheets feel colder. For a long time, I stayed on my side of the bed. Habit is a rigorous master.

Night, as couples know, is a sweet time. You're meeting, sharing in the unconscious world. You work through, side by side, what is too difficult to work through consciously. You make order out of what is bothering you or disturbing you. In sleep you are sharing an intimate time as you hold a safe place for one another. So, the very few times early on that I dreamed of Richard, I was relieved and excited to see him. In each dream I hugged him, looked over his body, and fell into him as I always had, with the top of my head reaching the soft crevice of the nape of his neck, nestled in his arms. I would meet him at the ocean and we would wade in the surf together. I would hold Richard's hand and just look at him, taking in every detail of his face as I had done in life, memorizing every detail of his face; I was so glad to see him. In the morning I would wake up feeling happy.

But most mornings I woke in deep grief, my sheets wet with tears. "It's all right, Boo," he would have said. I could almost feel his strong body melding into mine, rocking and comforting me as I cried again, wanting my old life back.

One morning I sat somberly in the predawn, sipping my coffee. The armchair embraced me like a well-worn glove while a fire crackled, and the morning held me briefly in the comfort of familiarity. We had sat together like that in morning conversation about life thousands of times, ever since our college days. Minutes before I had settled, I had shuffled into the kitchen, barely awake, grabbed the coffee decanter and filled it with enough water to make a full pot. I routinely reached for our two favorite mugs, just as I had thousands of previous mornings, and set them side by side on the counter while I waited for the coffee to finish. Then I stared at the two mugs. *What was I doing?* I grimaced as the sudden reality knot in my stomach cinched, and I drew in my breath as I remembered that things had changed.

"I don't want to live like this!" my inner child screamed in a tantrum. "I want my life, the one that begins by drinking coffee with my husband and watching the sunrise over Mount Diablo from our bed. I want that safe feeling as I drive up the hill to our home knowing he is inside working at his desk, waiting for me until I can bounce in and tell him about my day. I want to feel the ground under my feet."

I realized that it was in the small things, the rituals you create with your partner, the ways you "be" together that are the most meaningful and are the nuances of your relationship. These small things drive home what you are missing most as grief takes over: drinking morning coffee together before your respective days begin, washing dishes, curling your feet together in bed at night, passing the toothpaste back and forth and talking while it dribbles down your face. We take these small experiences for granted when we live together for twenty-five years and think we have a lifetime left. You just assume you'll keep having more of them and that they'll go on forever. We all live thinking we will never die, and I was no different. I was asleep, thinking that Richard would always be here with me.

That morning as I sat in my kitchen lost in thought, my thoughts muddled, tacking between memories and lists. There was so much to do, but as the sky widened to daylight, I noticed the absence of morning fog, and was reminded of a similar sky on a day when I had a goal and Richard, knowing it was going to be rough for me, supported me through it. That had been when we ran the San Francisco marathon together in July 1995. As we assembled for the start on the Golden Gate Bridge at sunrise, we had been surprised to see a bright, clear sky, not a good omen at the start of a four-hour, hillscaped run, at least in July it isn't. We knew the day was going to be a hot one! At the last minute Richard decided to run the distance with me. He hadn't really trained by doing the "long runs," but having completed two previous marathons in almost half the time mine would take, he figured he was in good enough shape and could manage. He ran almost every day back then, averaging about thirty miles per week.

I was so grateful to have him running beside me. I'll never forget his long stride as I ran a step behind, off his shoulder, and he encouraged me by saying, "All right, Kris! You're doing great, just six miles to go, you're going to make your goal of eight-and-a-half minute miles!" Because he was slightly ahead of me, he could only hear my exhausted groan in response. I was struggling. As he turned and saw the look on my face, he good-heartedly clapped his hands and said, "All right, new strategy! We finish this run!" *Just finish.* I hit the infamous wall and felt like I was dragging ten thousand pounds to the end, but we held hands as we ran the last lap on the track to the finish. The next day I moved slowly, creakily. Richard didn't feel much better, but we laughed as our kids looked at us with dismay and asked us why we would do something that hurt so bad. Good question, we said.

Now as I finished drinking my coffee, those words of his - "New strategy: Just finish." - rang through my head. They had had a powerful effect on me and I considered how to connect that insight to my new life. Challenging our capacity to be flexible and shifting our ideas about expectation were the tools Richard used to get me across the finish line. Just as in the marathon, I saw that my mind-set had to shift as I created a new strategy for life. That included succumbing fully to the emotional response of loss.

The beauty of grief is its clarity. What we have control over in our lives is not what happens, but we do have control over the choices we make after things happen. I had lived in denial of death and under the illusion that all would be stable and predictable in the safety net of our love. There had never been an obstacle Richard and I could not tackle together or a challenge we couldn't overcome. I had lived a life of affirmation alongside a man who became the foremost "happiness expert" in the world, and I was his wife. Would it have been easier to crawl into our empty bed with antidepressants and a fifth of vodka and disappear into the sadness? Maybe. But my daughters were looking to me for strength. I also knew I wanted to honor Richard by living for both of us. And, deep down, I knew that happiness is something we choose. It is lived in moments, moment to moment, like a strand of pearls. And I knew I'd rather be happy than miserable, but sorrow had to be embraced with open arms first. I was not going to have one without the other for some time.

As I sat facing this void in the quiet of morning, feeling alone and isolated, trapped in the waves of my despair, one empty coffee mug sitting beside my full one, I realized I needed to let Grief in. I needed to surrender. Grief would lead me and I would move through it, no matter. There was no escape route as an option.

I said, "God, bring it on," and it came like a tsunami.

4.

MY BODY TAUGHT ME

Grief is a journey. It is a winding road along a coastline that takes you up to the edge of a cliff. It is a birth canal with thousands of pounds of pressure squeezing you from the inside. On my saddest days, it often started as a sound in a breath. I would drop to my knees as pain overwhelmed me. I felt a deep, penetrating force – a contraction. I wanted it out. "Get out of my body," I would cry. I would lie on the floor in a primal scream, letting myself be as loud as I could, almost to the precipice, until the emotion was expelled. Then breath would return, and I would feel my heart in my chest, *thump thump thump,* until it became calm.

The only time I can remember a sensation similar to this is when my children were born. The processes of birthing a child and grieving are strangely similar. My birthing cycle would begin as I separated in the physical realm from a man I loved my whole adult life. It is not unlike the separation of a mother and child at birth. One requires the body to open through pain, and the other requires the heart to open to love through the doorway of loss. Contractions of pain came in waves as grief took me to the deepest place inside. It was the same place I had found myself during the cycles of pain that also came in the contractions of natural childbirth many years earlier. Each announced separation, but also the creation of new life.

When I was pregnant with Jasmine and Kenna, Richard and I took Lamaze classes. I had seen how beautiful birthing could be in videos of women with doulas and friends around them. Yet, when all is said and done, the only process that gets a woman through natural childbirth is the one she designs for herself in the moment.

21

When it was my time, I did all that I knew I could do. I retreated inward as my uterus expelled outward. The contractions came in waves with little respite, and I went deep into them as they came. I floated on the surface until the pain increased and the intensity took me to a different place. There was a universe inside, a dark but not scary place deep within. Instinctively, a contraction would begin, and as the pain increased I would open my knees, letting them fall to the side as my breath allowed me to follow a thread. By going into the pain, I became one with the source and open to life. Even though the pain was present with me and I with it, it did not consume me or keep me from experiencing each moment. There was stillness, and there was peace.

At the start of each contraction I would close my eyes and repeat words long familiar to me, a mantra: "Open to it. Surrender, trust and accept." While my fear would clench me into a fetal position, my wisdom allowed my legs to relax and open. Richard had looked at me so lovingly, wishing he could trade places with me yet knowing there was little he could do besides support my journey through it. He was right there at my side, holding my space. I felt myself drop into the abyss as I breathed, disappearing into this place at its highest intensity. I would go deep inside and return from the depth of the ocean floor with a gasping breath, only to dive in and surface again.

Now, so many years later, my world had been pulled apart. When I finally surrendered to the first wave of grief, it was to this same place that I returned, where life had been created and I trusted would be again.

When that first wave came, I knew I had experienced something like it before. My experience taught me that opening and surrendering to it would become my process. I decided to go all the way into whatever feelings came, swiftly and furiously, just as my birth contractions had taken me so naturally into this process. There was no mistaking it. I was in labor. Grief consumed me, as did the feeling that I had denied myself years of emotional expression. I didn't know how to brace myself against the bigness of these feelings, so I didn't try.

As my process deepened, I designed my days differently to make room for the waves of grief, to allow myself the space and time to go in as well as to come out of these mind-body-spirit waves. I would spend long hours in silence. I had no stimulus ... no radio, no television. I was selective in my reading, careful not to read books on "how" to do the grief process because there is no "right" process. Grief is its own teacher. I read instead from Kahlil Gibran and I read from the Bible. Eventually, I added books written by Pema Chodron, Melody Beattie, and Eckhart Tolle and Louise Hay. I read poetry. Exercise helped. Hiking and fresh air were really good for me, even when I was low. Sometimes I would sit on the floor listening to music and just let my body move. I was sensitive to all voices. Many different things triggered me: song lyrics, the world news, and the words of every story. Stories of loss especially held deep pain for me. For the first time in my life that I could remember, my story was the saddest of all.

After the girls left for school, I would lie in bed or on the floor and allow myself just to be wherever I happened to be emotionally. I breathed. I checked in. I noticed where my body held tension and I began to identify my body's language, often spoken through pain. I allowed my body's intelligence to show me the way out.

I remember one morning episode when I cried and screamed and kicked my legs. I beat the bedroom pillows, brushing aside the irony that they had become a sensitive subject between Richard and me. I was very particular about certain things. I used to become annoyed with Richard for using these beautiful silk pillows from India to support his knees. The pillows were decorative and meant to add ambience to our bed. For years I would pull them out from under him and he would look at me with a sheepish grin. But now, after beating and tossing them hard to the floor, I collapsed in tears, holding the pillows tenderly to my cheek, cherishing how he had lain on them, berating myself for how foolish I had been. *If only I had known.* Then I allowed grief to open me. I breathed. I cried again. I felt wasted. My body thanked me for letting it all out by replacing tension with peace. The pain had subsided. I rose and washed the salt from my face. And, my day began.

As I surrendered more and more to the grief and to my tears, my body began to change as well. It was strange. Something shifted and a youthful vitality returned. I looked years younger. I visited a massage therapist twelve weeks after my first surrender. She exclaimed, "Wow, Kris! I have never seen your neck so loose and your shoulders have completely opened in the back. Have you been doing a lot of yoga or something?"

Slowly, I would come to see that grief is the plow that clears the field for harvest. Without going through the emotional response to loss that is inevitable, there would be no joy for me. I knew I was a person of joy. My instincts told me there was no way to get back to that part of me without tilling the soil and allowing nature to clear the path for new growth. I was no longer holding life with the tight grip of fear. I was fully expressed for the first time in my adult life – as I spent hours a day crying. Just as a forest reseeds itself through fire, so does our spirit awaken and discover new life energy. As the massage therapist remarked, the results were actually visible.

My body was teaching me that grief was my friend, not my enemy, because it allowed me the healthy means to express the pain inside me. Some might say that grief and depression are the same, that they express a distinction without a difference, but that is wrong. Grief is different from depression. It is the emotional response to the pain and agony of separation, whereas depression is what happens when these emotions are pushed down and unexpressed. I became more adept at anticipating and surrendering sooner to the waves as they crashed upon me. I learned to read my emotions by the signals my body was giving. At first it was hours a day, but over time the cycles shortened. I would sometimes have reprieve days, often two or three-day cycles, before grief would return. And when it did, each wave would pass in and out, always leaving me with a sense of peace.

Intuitively, I understood that listening to my body and how it talked to me would be my path back to a new life. I also knew I needed to have stillness. I needed to create time and space for just being quiet – mindful only of my breath and where I could allow all those feelings of confusion, regret, fear, longing, and anger to surface and be expelled through grief. I learned I didn't have to be afraid of where my feelings might lead me, because it was all inside me. During even the toughest of those moments I would feel my husband beside me, like he had been during the birth of our children. Like on that hot marathon day and hundreds of other times – coaxing me forward, encouraging me to conquer pain, and loving me no matter what. I believed that he was there to guide me through grief – I felt his presence.

Creating the space to move in and out of whatever came was essential to my healing. I learned to surrender and to allow mind, body, and spirit to integrate. I discovered that as a gust of wind forces the door open wide, so did grief open my heart.

5.

LIVING PRESENTLY

The beauty of grief is presence. Grieving is a very individual and layered process. On my better days, I experienced a calm well-being. I noticed the skies never looked so beautiful. I could feel Richard's love all around me. I deeply missed him and the full life together I always thought we would continue to share. Yet each step I took, I felt somehow, I was stepping more into me.

But for a long time, there were too many of those other days. I knew all too well that every step forward I took I was leaving Richard behind and acknowledging a life already complete. Small things felt overwhelming – like taking his name off our checking accounts and credit cards. Everywhere I turned in the house there were signs that he had lived there. His swim trunks and goggles still hung on the hook outside where he had left them. His folded shirts sat at the bottom of the laundry basket, his shoes in the closet. I called his voice-mail just to hear his voice, because I so ached for conversation with him. I took walks with his mother. We cried and laughed. We tried to make some sense of it all and comfort each other.

Physical signs – scuffs on the floor, the odd handwritten notes, the groceries Richard had bought – this evidence that he had been *here* – those little things brought me down hard. After a few months, it became necessary to throw away the dated products he had purchased at the Safeway. I never thought I would cry from tossing out a jar of jelly. It seemed impossible and so unfair that with each little action I was surely erasing the one person who gave to me endlessly and who had made my life so happy.

The future felt daunting because it held a new life without him. So much of my life had been fixed, had been certain, and the ordinary rhythms of our life together now seemed precious, exciting even. But I realized that I was sinking into a habit of longing that I had to break before it broke me. I knew I needed to step back into Life.

Grief has a way of thrusting you into the present. When you have just been bereaved and are barely surviving the loss of your loved one, it is natural to go into memory where you are most comfortable, just as it is natural to be terrified of your future. I was in such deep pain at the beginning that I found I could only handle the past and the future in small doses. I learned to acclimate to the present moment because that was the only place where I could live with a sense of equilibrium. So, I learned to live in the midline of my life – in my present, just where I was – with my past to my left and my future to my right.

When you live in the present your mind is not busy. It is a quiet yet brilliantly clear space because it is uncluttered. You're not thinking of anything you have to do, or distracted by anywhere you have to go; you are not allowing your thought to drift into the past that you miss or into the future you fear. You are living in alignment with the moment. When grief catches you, you feel the wave as you roll into it. It is a space where you exist, right now, where life finds you, wherever you are. It is a place of safety that is also shared by the adventurous. It is a concentrated state that is known by rock climbers and rafters and skiers and anyone else who puts themselves into dangerous situations. There is a heightened state of awareness when you live presently; you see every crevice, you feel the fold of rock, the iron-gray air, the numinous texture of the physical world. Loss, after all, can be a dangerous place, too. The future is a Grand Canyon of vast and unknown openness. And so, I surrendered to "now." I found that whenever I brought my attention back to the moment, I was not overwhelmed.

For the time being, I would ride the river, understanding that it is a series of flow, of currents, rapids and calm. "It is what it is," Richard and

I used to tell our girls when explanation eluded us. Grief was a current I would not fight by trying to swim upstream. I would let it take me wherever it went. I determined to let each moment present itself and just be with that.

I surrendered to grief. I embraced the moment and its meaning. I learned how to live in it without resistance or escape. *Surrender, trust, accept, and receive* – a mantra I had learned years ago and that returned to me like a vessel to protect me even in the roughest storm.

Now it was time to trust that a gentle wind would carry me home.

6.

THERE IS LAUGHTER

Life is not all grief, all joy, or all of any one thing. Life is a mixture of all things. Grief has shown me that even in suffering there is laughter, and that laughter is a way back. Laughter is a healer. It is evidence that we are here now. It is a reminder that even if our world has been rocked off its axis, our *nature* is intact; while we may be fragile, we will come back.

I learned very early that laughter pulls us into the present, too. When we laugh, even when there is loss, it is like the sound of cracking ice. We are open to life and fully present to it. Laughter is all about the moment. Living presently is one of the most powerful survival techniques grief has shown me. Laughter is the ultimate release; it is surrender.

Deciding to commit my Richard's remains for cremation was the thing I dreaded most of all. I tried not to dwell on the transformation that would occur, but I couldn't stop myself. I was thinking about my beloved - whose eyes I had looked into, whose hands I had held, whose arms I had slept in for twenty-five years. His body would become ash, and he would be sent home to me in a tiny box. That stark reality was crushing, yet facing it was one of those things that had to be done, and I was the one to do it. So, I did the only thing I knew to do – I brought two close friends along to meet the "specialist" at the mortuary.

I knew what would be required: sign paperwork to have Richard's body transferred from the mortuary in New York, plan for his cremation, and select a box for his ashes. All of it made me shiver but I never expected this sad errand would leave us in tears – *of laughter*.

The day was typical of Bay Area winters – cold and wet, the gloom had already settled into my bones. The specialist greeted us.

His appearance was striking. He had carrot-orange hair reaching every which way as if he had barely made it out of bed. He wore a short-sleeved dress shirt that bloused over his extended belly, along with the kind of slacks my dad used to wear. He introduced himself and spoke an appropriately respectful expression of condolence that felt over-used and stale like hardened sourdough bread. He waved for us to have a seat around the table that was meant to resemble deep-polished wood but was instead vinyl veneer.

Fake flowers hung from a basket on the wall along with imitation oil paintings that reeked of bad taste and depression. Even the room was painted gray. The three of us must all have had the same thoughts because just then, he lifted his bushy eyebrows and said, in a tone that was deadpan, macabre, almost seductive, "Ladies, I'll be right back," and stepped out of the room to get some papers. My friends were watching to take my cue and, although I tried, I could not hold back. I had a vision of that classic TV comedy *The Munsters*. As the door closed I burst out laughing and my friends followed. We had a difficult time maintaining any composure after that. In fact, we laughed until we cried. It came naturally, and it felt really good.

A few weeks later my girlfriend Laura and I pulled up again to the mortuary entrance, this time to collect Richard's ashes. I had dreaded the day and had not slept well the night before. I turned to her and said, "I can't believe I am doing this." She shook her head and reached over and gave my hand a reassuring squeeze.

We walked inside and the director greeted us once more in that low, seductive voice as he thrust his damp hand into mine. In a dramatic whisper he said, "I'll be bringing him shortly." We sat again at the same round table and I suddenly felt quite nervous. My beloved was about to be handed to me in a box, like a trophy. Ten minutes later, the mortuary director returned carrying a green, synthetic velvet sack containing the box that held Richard's ashes inside. He took a seat and formally folded his hands with the box in front of him. "Would you like to make sure it's him?" he asked. I saw that he was dead serious. I could barely stifle a laugh.

I stared at him for a long moment before I responded, "And how do you propose I do that?"

"Oh, his name is right inside," he told me.

I replied, "Did you read it?"

He said, "Yes, it says Richard Carlson."

I bit my lip so I wouldn't laugh outright and said, "Well then, that's good enough for me. Hand him over." He slid the box to me, and I placed both hands around it protectively. Then I picked it up and cradled it lovingly in the crook of my arm as I signed the release form with my other hand before we left. But as we began to pull out of the parking space, I realized something wasn't right. I said, "Oh my God, Laura, stop this car!" I opened the green satchel and saw a black, shiny, plastic container, like the kind they use to store film. "I can't believe this!" I said as I stomped back in and demanded, "Where is the three-hundred-and-fifty-dollar oak box with gold trim that I selected and paid for? Richard Carlson does not belong in plastic!"

The gentleman walked away and returned about ten minutes later with the proper box, ashes properly transferred. I could hear Richard say, "Kris, c'mon, lighten up! Don't sweat the small stuff!" And he was right. Had I just heard myself say that my husband did not belong in *plastic?* I relaxed. I felt like I was in the middle of a Peter Sellers comedy. Sometimes you just have to laugh.

We took the box home. I tried to think of a place to store him that the girls would not have to constantly see to remind them of our sadness. I decided Richard's closet would be the best place. With Laura by my side, I took a framed family photo and a locket of his hair, then cut some pieces of my own and slipped them in the bag. I nestled the box on the top shelf around copies of some of Richard's books, an impromptu memorial and temporary resting place until we would commend Richard's ashes to the sea for all eternity. As I stepped off the stool to the floor, something fell from the top shelf. I reached down and picked up the baseball cap the girls had given Richard when they were little. "Number 1 Dad!" it read. Laura and I laughed out loud again. I said, "Of course, honey!" I placed the cap over the top of the box at a slightly roguish tilt. It made me chuckle whenever I thought about it. And whenever I did, I just felt better.

As that sad season pressed on, each day I would remind myself of the lessons of that day. I had let go of my thoughts, fears, and expectations of what terrible things might come, and was surprised, even buoyed by the healing power of laughter. When we open to the moment, every day holds surprise – the incoherence of sorrow, perhaps, but also the appearance of joy. I tried to remain an empty cup waiting to be filled. I learned things weren't all bad, even on my worst days. And I found that when I stayed present in the moment, I didn't have to look far to find a reason to smile. Laugh when the opportunity presents itself, something told me, because that is Spirit healing us, too.

Two

TRUST

… Life and Love Will Lead Me

7.

MY INNATE HEALER

Sometime after the first anniversary of Richard's death, my computer completely crashed and I was sure I had lost everything. I had kept a journal that first year that turned out to be four hundred pages long. I wasn't sure I could retrieve anything from my hard drive, but I knew that loss was nothing compared to what I had been through. By that time, I was so into "surrender to everything" that I was surprisingly relaxed – even though what might be lost were significant pieces of what became this book. I took a deep breath. I was submerged in my post-doctorate education in the classroom of life and realized there was a theme to the lessons I was to glean from my losses, and this was just another "test." I decided to wait until the computer technicians told me there was nothing to retrieve before I grieved again. It just seemed another lesson in "surrender, trust and accept." By then, I had put my life into such deep perspective that I trusted I would be okay, no matter what. And so, I did not fall apart although at some earlier part of my life I surely might have. Instead I waited, and although repairs were expensive, nothing was lost.

I realize now that I already had a glimmer of this same understanding that life would lead me during that first spring when my heart was so freshly broken open.

Our lives may be pierced by tragedies we half-understand, but I believe that suffering is what we have in common as human beings. Our life story is not about whether we are going to know sorrow and hardship, but *when*. Yet, my experience has shown me that we grow and deepen our awareness through struggle – this is why we have suffering; there can be no other reason. I didn't mean to, but before Richard passed I took for granted that my life was somehow charmed, and that our family had been touched by the beneficent hands of the Creator. Until then, ours had been doable hardships ... but then my time came.

When tragedy strikes, it is natural for us to call on our faith and reach deep inside ourselves for the answers. *Why did God do this?* I want to know. *What will happen to us now?* I am in question about almost all aspects of my life.

From the beginning, however, I knew that Richard's death was no spiritual accident. It was not a punishment, but a part of a much bigger design. There were times, though, I struggled with feeling abandoned, thinking cynically that God must have had an Alzheimer's moment at the timing of this, yet a wiser voice always returned swiftly to reassure me. I trusted that God had something in store for me and that this loss was supposed to count for something deeper for me, my girls, and for Richard, too. Like all humankind, this was *our* "something" to face. While none of this made that time any easier, instead of focusing on the event, I decided to trust that Life would lead me to the answers. Everything I needed would come to me at the right time, and I would heal.

As a girl, I loved to ride the roller coaster. I would raise my arms high above my head with a child's confidence that, despite my fear as the train on its seemingly endless winding and whipping tracks hurtled me through the ride, I was safe and that it would take me where I needed to go. Life is like that, too. Every day it keeps going and Life presents itself without missing a beat. I realized I could live in the uncertain and unknown so long as I believed that Life would come to me if I remained open to it.

I had already surrendered to what I could not control; all I needed was to be a willing participant in my life as it unfolded now.

Trust was the ladder – the structure – that helped me scale my mountain, and what I came to call my Innate Healer became the support. My Innate Healer had shown up when I trusted that I could reveal everything that I needed to heal and to get from one moment to the next. It was about tuning into my divinity – and by this, I mean my own deep reserve of wisdom, knowledge, intuition and faith – and allowing that to flow through me like a river taking me with the current.

I believe that everyone has an innate healer; it is the capacity to tune into a deeper part of ourselves and intuit a process of healing that comes from the culmination of all our life experience. It is what we have learned to be true, honest, and real, and to reveal from inside us. All we need is trust to know that when we need it, it is there. When I looked back at my life and what it had already taught me, I found guidance and sustenance. My past experiences helped me realize that I would find my way – that grief would pass and that I could live again in the hard margin of the world.

We spend so much of our energy protecting ourselves from the discomfort of pain. Now, with the experience of Richard's death, I found myself falling back into the liquid calm of memory, revisiting a difficult time in my life that I was surprised to find had prepared me to cope and live through loss. It is a gift to be able to see that the random succession in our experiences, as children, young adults, and beyond, somehow all unfolds into a meaningful sequence.

***

Looking back, I saw how I had climbed peaks of pain and disillusionment early in my life.

I come from a family with strong religious roots. One of my earliest spiritual experiences happened when I was five. My mother had just dropped me off at summer Bible school and my brother was taken to a different class. I was terrified. I knew no one and played on the swings alone.

Later, we all sat at the teacher's feet as she read a story about a man called Jesus born the son of God: "You are never alone. Jesus loves you more than your mommy and daddy. He is always with you and he is your friend." I felt a shiver, then a warm tingling all over. It was as if I were suddenly embraced in the warmest hug.

She finished and the other children ran off to play. I remained with my hands folded in my lap, chin raised high, and my legs crossed under my pinafore dress. Tears rolled down my cheeks. "Kristine, what's wrong, dear?" the teacher asked.

I responded in a voice that must have sounded very adult, "I felt him. He's here."

She looked at me and for a moment she didn't understand. And then she smiled and said, "That's wonderful. You carry him with you, just like he's in your pocket and let him love you always." I knew, even then, I had been touched.

I began to talk with Jesus and my heart would soar. He carried me many times through my childhood fears. I loved church and I always listened intently. As I grew older, I became annoyed at the people who fell asleep during sermons. Didn't they want to know how to be a better person, too? I hung on every word and interpretation. I studied and followed the Ten Commandments. Of course, I messed up now and then. Sometimes I would forget to pray for forgiveness. But I felt loved and guided by God from deep within.

And so it went, until I got older and the stakes were higher. In time, the tropes of my faith ceased to inspire me, and questions about how to be a good person became harder to answer. My relationship with God shifted, a separation that began when I was fourteen. When I was ready to rediscover the role of faith in my life, I was twenty. Richard was at my side by then, and we would search widely. Those years in between sometimes felt like a thousand deaths, but I learned how we can create our lives, if we choose.

During high school I had a boyfriend who was a popular upperclassman. One night as we parked up in the skyline drive to make out, he grew aggressive. He started pulling off my panty hose and pulling at my clothes even as I tried to get him to stop. I was a cross-country runner at the time and was strong; I managed to leg-press some distance between us but not long before he ejaculated all over my now-bare legs. He started crying and apologizing. I told him to take me home. I was crying, too. Good Christian girl that I was, I imagined that God had watched this, and that somehow it had been my fault. Even though I had narrowly escaped rape, my trust in men had been assaulted, my naïve innocence shattered.

When I walked into my house, a visiting relative saw my streaked mascara and swollen eyes. She asked what was wrong. My parents were asleep, so I told her what happened. Her eyes narrowed with disgust and her response would accelerate my plummet into a destructive place I had already started to visit. "You know, Kristine," she said, "if you're inviting those kinds of things, then you are already sinning in God's eyes." Humiliated and confused, my worst fear validated, I wanted to die.

I now spiraled into deep despair and guilt. Like many girls at my age who find tragedy in the dark pond of Perfection, I stuffed down and repressed my emotions as I discovered "coping" in the cycle of binge eating and bulimic purging. The speed with which an addiction devastates is frightening. The stealing of change from my parents' drawer to purchase bags of chips and cookies and ice cream (which made everything come up easier); the hideous retching noises while they were at work and I would be alone in the house; the image of myself splayed naked and annihilated on the bathroom floor; all of this returned to me now during this time of bereavement settling over me like a witch's cape.

During those years I was also training for varsity cross-country. Driven to keep up with our team, I thought I would run faster if I were thinner. I was bingeing upwards of ten times a day. Finally, during a track meet, I collapsed. Not even the doctor saw through to my secret. "Your electrolyte balance was all messed up from overtraining," he said. He recommended Gatorade and vitamins.

I went home and for the first time realized I was killing myself. That night, I walked into my parents' bedroom. They lay in bed watching TV. I sat at the foot of their bed and said, "I have something to tell you." And then I told them everything.

The next day, I saw the doctor again and he told me I had a disorder called anorexia nervosa. He couldn't understand how this had happened to me. I was pretty, young, athletic, an excellent student. He took my hand and said, "You need to stop eating so much and you have to stop vomiting." I was fifteen and I thought; *Jeez, no kidding.*

I knew my parents loved me and would do anything for me, but even the doctor didn't really know what to do because little was known about eating disorders at that time. My parents couldn't have understood the depth of the problem I had because it barely had a name.

And that was that. I knew I was on my own.

I switched from cross-country to modeling, which helped take away some of my feeling of athletic inadequacy, but it was a long climb out of that swamp. My classmates never guessed that the "perfect girl" was a mess inside. My parents thought I was instantly cured. I wasn't. Instead, I learned for myself how to delve into my own psychology to identify my emotional triggers and learn how to cope better with stress, body image, and my emerging sexuality. I had to find my own willpower, and to learn to talk with myself. I changed my relationship with food, eating more frequently and slowly while feeling and tasting each bit. I discovered I could never sit down with a box or bag of anything. And, I had to limit the amount of time spent alone.

*you have to burn yourself
down to the ground*

I continued to struggle with my insecurities, demons, and urges, and many times I won. When I lost, I felt like a failure, but the cycle would have a start point and I could slip back out again. It was always three steps forward and two steps back as my cycle lessened from ten times a day to two or three times a month. Slowly, bulimia released me from its grip.

I was mostly recovered four years later when I fell in love with Richard. We met as students at Pepperdine University. He was tall, strong, and so handsome. I was eighteen and he was twenty. We quickly became inseparable. One night as we sat holding hands, I could barely look into his eyes as I summoned the courage to tell him my secret. He looked at me intently and with such kindness, said, "I know girls who do that." Then he smiled and peered at me through gentle eyes. "I wouldn't imagine it being very healthy long-term though." As I cried, he continued, "You know, Kris, there are few people in this world who go through life without their demons. It takes courage to face yours and as long as you do, love means I love all of you."

They say it takes as long to recover from an eating disorder as the duration of the disorder itself, and that was true. At twenty-one years of age I rounded the final bend in my recovery. We were married soon after.

As weeks after Richard's passing lengthened into months, I would feel a heaviness that began in my arms and then would course through me as the finality of his absence set in. Only after I again found myself in deep pain did I recognize what a blessing it had been for me to recover from that eating disorder. Having once designed my own process for healing, I could draw on that useful perspective now. I could have easily slipped back into the very repressed place I knew and remembered. But I had learned how important it is to find healthy ways to express emotion and why – just as I did when I learned to embrace grief – you have to burn yourself down to the ground. As a teenager, I hadn't had a lot of help or support with recovery. My parents did the best they could for the times we were in. I know now that repression numbs you and only leads to despair and depression.

At the time of Richard's death, I became very aware that I had the potential to slip back into every old destructive habit from my past. I realized this as a friend brought me together with another recent widow. I met with her to lend some sense of camaraderie and support. Over lunch, I noted that she ordered a cocktail. I thought how easy it would have been for me to slide back into bulimia, or to numb out through drinking. The first four months I didn't have so much as a glass of wine. I wanted my feelings to be real and I did not want to be under the influence of any depressant or stimulant or prescription drug.

This time, I definitely chose a different route and allowed myself to feel my life and those painful emotions in a beautiful, healthy way of full expression. As I allowed myself to ease into my sadness, in softer waves my vision would blur with tears. In all the years before Richard's death, I very rarely cried for myself. What always stopped me was the thought that if I couldn't be happy, then no one could. What, really, did I have to cry about anyway? I'd think. And then I would go and do something to distract myself.

Somehow, I felt unworthy of tears because I had been so richly blessed. It seemed that during my married years, I had forgotten the lessons I had learned from my eating disorder over two decades before. I remembered meeting a psychologist, who during that fragile time when I was still in recovery, attempted to teach me how to cry. He would say that every tear I shed was for a thousand years of sorrow. I was young and didn't know what he meant by that. I do now.

My past experience with an eating disorder showed me that life really does prepare us. Every loss, every hard time, isn't for naught. Everything in life, I learned, gets us ready for the next thing. My history with an eating disorder played a huge role in my healing now, for without it I would never have known how to access my innate healer, my intuition and wisdom. I had confidence that my capacity to move through darkness would help me to find the bliss of my own light.

I didn't know that about myself until Richard died, that I had that in me. I saw that I would heal because I had healed before. I had already survived a very difficult passage in life. I had found my own way once, so I knew I could do this. I stood in grateful amazement that a painful episode that was long ago left behind in what now seemed like another life could unexpectedly reappear and reverberate, that the past was a protective shoulder I could lean on to guide me to the future.

Like the little girl who rode the roller coaster and trusted it would carry her to safety, we come around the curve of suffering and rebuild our lives.

8.

ANGELS SHOW UP

Grief is a road each of us travels as an individual, for we each respond differently to loss and have a different path to healing. Nevertheless, we all need friends to hold space for our grief and provide a safe container for us during our healing time.

Few of us ever know what our community really is until we are in crisis. In the march of our busy, hurried lives – managing home, family, work, and everything else – we may sometimes feel we never have a half hour to call our own, to delve deep into friendship and community. We either assume community is there or tell ourselves we don't need it. I was no exception. Losing Richard showed me how wrong I was.

Friends and strangers can show up in a variety of ways when tragedy strikes. It is up to us to let them in and make the most of the opportunity to deepen bonds. Most everyone is called to his or her strengths in these scenarios. Some friends offer help in concrete ways with small things that were once easy and automatic but now seem overwhelming. I was frustrated and stymied by stupid things – turning ahead the clocks on our wall appliances or fixing the router on the computer. I would have to learn to do things for myself that I didn't want to learn, and learning them was a stinging reminder that Richard would never again be here to do them. I had to learn to swallow my pride to reveal basic areas of ignorance and ask for help.

Some friends just sit with you in your pain because, often, that is all a person can do. Some know what to say and what not to say. During those first hours, when I felt I could capsize like a wreck rising and falling in a churning sea, one friend stabilized me with a gesture and a few words. Laura took my chin in her hand so that she had my full attention. "Kris, honey," she said, looking me square in the eyes, "you will not go through this alone. I will be with you every step of the way. You are not alone."

Simple, and perhaps obvious, but it was exactly what I needed to hear. I knew she meant it, and she lived up to her words in spades. The love of friends is the tonic that helps heal the wounds of separation.

I also found strength in cards and letters. They poured in from around the world. I had not realized how much a shared story or memory, an insight or reflection, lifts the bereaved.

I knew from the beginning that I wasn't going to be able to do it all on my own. It was one of the only times in my life I had to let go and allow other people to take care of me. I surrendered to my vulnerability and trusted that my friends would show up. It was a leap from being one of the supporters to being supported. I don't call on people easily. Richard and I supported each other. I remember how, even after the New Year's mudslide eleven months before he passed, when we needed our friends, we didn't think to call. "Why didn't you?" they asked us later.

So now I did. I learned to ask, and it strengthened me. During that long, long time when I just couldn't find the ground, I called on friends. "Just walk me, just rock me," I asked them. There were times I would cry hard, even well after the immediate shock had passed. I needed someone to just hold my space. One morning I called our friends Rich and Yvonne. It was May. Richard's birthday was coming up. I was crying so hard I couldn't speak. "I am on my way," Rich said. He came right over and got on top of the bed with me and just held me like a father holds a child while I cried big, heavy tears, my body clenching in and out like a fist. He just held me and let me know he was there, and never tried to comfort me out of it. It was just what I needed. My deepest grief happened that spring, when the reality that Richard was never coming home, never going to hold me again, crashed over me and sank in. During those first months, Richard had still felt present.

Some people who knew me were surprised that my process wasn't faster. Some friends expected me to survive this with nothing but grace. At times I felt sad that everyone else got to move on while I lived in two worlds at once, learning to live in the new while missing the old. Sometimes that felt like a lot to hold. I told myself that God was breaking me and my world in order to remake me. Try telling that to your friends.

And so, there were awkward moments as I re-found my footing. I rode the fluidity and discontinuity of my emotions like a hot lava flow. I was certain only that we each grieve in our own way and time, and that I would ask for and take from others the same love and support I would give if the situation were reversed. I always believed myself to be a kind and thoughtful person. Now, for the first time in my life, I could be selfish and inconsiderate. There were many times when I canceled appointments just before I was due to arrive, saying, "I'm sorry, I can't be there. I am having a really sad day today."

What I needed to survive came to me moment by moment.

Most understood but others did not, and that was okay. I was sitting at lunch one day with a friend when she looked at me alarmed and asked, "Are you okay?" I had begun to cry. "Did I say something to make you sad?"

"No," I told her. "It's not you! Richard died. Did you forget? I'm crying because I'm still crying!" Similarly, Jazz and Kenna would come home from school and tell me they felt like screaming when their friends would ask them, "What's wrong?" What the hell did they think was wrong?

We need our friends and they are, almost universally, wonderful. They show up in a million different meaningful ways for us. It's only natural that they would want to try to "fix" something that is totally out of their control. Our angels fear they may trigger our sorrow or that they are failing in their job as a friend if we are very sad in their presence. Good friends want to help, but in my case, I didn't need to be rescued. I didn't want to be distracted. I needed to feel held and supported to be wherever I was at the moment. Fortunately, I could be honest with most of them about that.

There are times in life when the only thing we can offer someone else is our presence. My best moments came when a friend was simply *there* to hold space and receive my feelings, in all their depth and bigness. Most people have never been shown how to do this. Grief is an opportunity for you to not only receive love and wisdom from friends, but it is as well an opportunity for your friends to grow in their capacity to listen deeply. I noticed that those who were helping us through loss began to live more awake themselves; empathy and acts of kindness tend to recue us from the self-absorption that can happen in our daily lives. I know because I saw changes in some of my friends who were nearest in my journey.

My most healing companions were simply the best listeners. One dear friend stayed by my side long after my other friends moved back into their busy lives. Even today, T.J. calls nearly every morning just to check in, goes on long walks with me, listens to my stories about Richard, and hears me on my low days. There would be days after I had emptied out when I would break from the deep and overwhelming sadness and even find laughter. On those days my voice sounded like old joyful Kris. I spoke with one friend on the phone who cried because she was so happy to hear my cheerful spirit return. It takes almost as much courage to stay voluntarily in someone's life and witness their pain as it does for the bereaved to endure it. It would be so easy to fly away. Our angels don't. They stand in our pain with us, and let us just *be* with it without changing what it is.

Friends will come and go as part of the messy process. There are people who can be in grief with you and can hold that space with you and there are some who can't. I was lucky to have a team around me. But even the most well-meaning friends and family may be uncomfortable with grief and impatient with your expression of it.

In February a friend came for a weekend visit. She was disturbed to find Kenna spending so much time in her room. "Get her out of her room," she urged repeatedly. "It's not good for her." I had to explain that we were in our own process here, that maybe our feelings were not something she could understand but that she could not do this for us. If Kenna needed to be in her own room, so be it. I would continue to check in on her, but I had to respect her process, and so had my friend. Judging us was not helpful.

There will always be people who will want to try and "make" you happy or just "wish" you back to your old self without understanding either that happiness can come only *after* you have journeyed through all the grief, or that grief *will* change you. Just as some were not comfortable with me in my pain, I discovered there were others who were disturbed to see me begin to emerge from the protective cocoon that deep grief can be. They were afraid to see me leave this place where they had grown to love me most. But you can't stay in deep grief forever. You're meant to stay in that place only long enough to heal and be whole.

There is a community among those with shared experience. Beginning in the spring, I started to expand my network of friends to include other single women and men, some widowed, some divorced, and some further along into their transitions into new lives than I. All of them were diverse and interesting, and many were quite colorful, very different from my tight suburban circle. Meeting them was wonderful, yet in the beginning it made my married friends uneasy to see me going out so much. I had to reassure them that they were not losing me to another life. They were releasing me to find my way through this new life that I didn't ask for but had to find a way to live in.

Transitions, I found, were hard for all of us. Just as we need our friends during loss, they need us, too. Richard's death upset a deep and ingrained dynamic. There was a healing process for all of us. Together we discovered the only wrong way to go through grief is alone.

I used to think of community as a church or a special subculture. I didn't think I had one. I just thought I had developed many, many friends. Now I know that God manifests in all the people who show up to see you through. It was difficult for the three of us to go from being an envied family to suddenly being pitied. It was odd to go from being the one who was strong to being the one who needed to be held. There is separateness in always being so strong. I never realized that I was holding my friends, and even the world in a sense, at arm's length by not exposing myself fully.

Fortunately, there was no hiding my humanity in this experience. I learned how to ask, because I had to. I learned how to take, because I needed to. I said yes to the offer of support, because it was my time. It was like Pay It Forward; you pass it on. And when that need was over, I would become part of the circle of healing again. Independence would come … but not yet. I allowed myself to see the value in friends – those with whom I had shared experience. In time, I learned to move easily between both independence and friendship. I now *know* what community is.

9.

SEEING CONTRAST AND ILLUSION

I met a woman not long after Richard died who had found her husband in a chair, gone. She had taken her children to school in the morning and when she returned, she found him. After speaking with her, I realized that I was not an average person living a conventional American life. I started in grief healing at a different place, having many valuable tools in my belt. Having struggled with an eating disorder, I understood my own psyche. I knew all about the importance of self-expression. I knew that anger is the reverse side of depression. I already knew how to meditate. I understood the importance of living in the moment – not planning too far ahead, and about the connection between our emotions and our physical bodies.

I had had a tremendous spiritual education, even as losing Richard stretched me like a rubber band, putting all my tools to the test. I could see that this woman would go through her journey in a different way than I did. She was in denial, and I never was. She was going about her life as if her husband was on a trip, as though he was still here. She was staying busy, not allowing herself to sit still. That way, she wouldn't have to think about her loss, or feel her life. I didn't do that. I was never in denial. I knew that denial would be a dangerous place for me to enter. I feel that we are here to experience human life at a very deep level, that we are meant to build something in our souls that goes with us at the end of our lives, and that we cultivate that on a spiritual plane. When I would meet and speak with other new widows, many of them talked about living that first year in a fog. That never happened with me. I became clear very quickly.

I know now how important it is to do spiritual work when life is good. That is the time to learn, seek, jump in, and to understand what nourishes you. Diving into a passionate interest or practice teaches you so much about yourself and that associated interest is going to serve you when life isn't going so well. These will be our healthy tools and they will be what we refer to in a number of ways while surviving loss. Today, I want to tell people not to wait, but to do their inner work and prepare. Letting go is the hardest part of loss. If you practice letting the small stuff go, day by day, this will help you when the stakes are higher and life throws you a curveball and the big stuff happens.

If my eating disorder prepared me for much of what was to come, then my life with Richard prepared me for the rest. When I met Richard, I experienced a spiritual reawakening, and we chose to dive into our spirituality as seekers. We began to answer the more complicated questions about how to live in the world as spiritual beings embracing a broader and more Unitarian approach to spirituality. I was no longer alone. I began to feel worthy of God's love again.

Richard, always an avid reader like his dad, was already reading books by Dale Carnegie, Spencer Johnson, Wayne Dyer, Norman Cousins, Ram Dass, Stephen Levine, Roger Kipling, Richard Bach, and many others. In his teen years, his journey was inspired by his tennis career, driven by the desire to keep a mental edge, using self-help techniques such as the power of positive thinking and creative visualization. Then, I think, he just fell in love with human psychology and the concept of self-empowerment that came out of the new era known as pop psychology that later flowed into the New Age movement. All of it was a part of a whole new world of spirituality to explore.

It was a fertile period of internal growth for each of us. I was recovering from my eating disorder; Richard was quitting tennis and letting go of a life dream to become a world-class player. We were in a period of self-discovery then. Our twenties were a deeply awakening spiritual time for us. As a couple finding a groove together, we soaked up Eastern philosophy and applied its principles to creating our lives together. We read books together: Kahlil Gibran, Shakti Gawain, Florence Scovel Shinn, and many others that fit into our spare time along with our university studies. We meditated daily and shared a morning practice of gratitude. We were exposed to new ideas and philosophies. By the time I was twenty-five I was familiar with rebirthing, astrology, palm reading; I had studied Christianity, Buddhism, and transformational meditation. I knew how to calm myself and how to go inside myself to learn and to heal. I was already a young married woman, newly pregnant with Jasmine, when Richard and I traveled for the first time to southern India to see Satya Sai Baba, whose teachings we had discovered through our readings and who became our spiritual teacher.

Having a guru will strike some as strange or exotic, and it was an unexpected turn in our path, but our guru became an integral part of our spiritual grounding. We studied and looked into so many different areas, and our awareness deepened as Richard studied for his Master's and Ph.D. degrees in psychology. For his writing he searched for the commonality of all paths to God, the golden thread in all religions. Richard had a complex understanding yet also had a way of expressing himself through a simple and easy language that both children and adults could comprehend.

In his books he would draw on his psychological training, see the links between diverse spiritual principles, and bring those into his work and see beyond them. In this way, he brought his readers through the back door into a form of spirit that transcended religion but was pure common sense and all heart. He had discovered the common thread was love, and that love transcends the boundaries of secular thought. He focused on teaching about how personal responsibility for one's happiness was necessary to creating a peaceful life of joy. He knew that if his readers could be kinder and gentler, they would feel more compassionate and better about themselves and this would have a ripple effect. Those positive good feelings would spill into their lives, creating inner peace and harmony. Through much soul searching and many levels of understanding, through years of seeking and years of reflection, he brought these teachings and psychological understandings to everyone. Satya Sai Baba had been instrumental in showing him how.

Sai Baba was a powerful part of our journey together. I always knew that if I ever needed a loving and healing environment, I would head straight to the safety of Baba. It was rather like having an emergency plan if there is a fire; I would understand more being in his presence. Throughout the winter following Richard's passing, I had been reading his journal from the time when he and I had visited the ashram eighteen years before. We were young but already well into our spiritual journey. It was a magical time, and we experienced a way of life I wanted to live again. It took a lot of courage to make that trip the first time, especially with the obstetrician advising me not to do it.

Now I needed to tap into my well of courage again to make a long journey so early into this life after Richard. But it seemed to me that this is where I could show my daughters how spiritual signs can teach us about our direction, and that everyone and everything comes into our path for a reason. There are always obstacles to overcome and Baba says, "We must dive deep for the pearl." So, I decided we would go to India during the girls' spring break. We would step out of our safe haven. I hoped the girls would feel the fatherly and divine feminine love of Sai Baba, and connect with the spiritual in a place inside themselves where they could feel Richard the way I did. I hoped they would see that death is not permanent, but a transition instead from form to formless. These were big concepts for two young girls, who had almost no experience with death, to take in. I hoped that in the loving embrace of the ashram and in the soft, light air of India each of us would breathe through our fears about life without Richard in human form.

The practical, rational part of me knew it was just a little crazy to pack us up and go all the way to southern India to an ashram and back in less than seven days. Our dear friend Naomi, who had visited Sai Baba many times, made the trip with us to help negotiate the ashram. I wouldn't have traveled such a distance completely on my own at this time. It was exactly four months to the day of Richard's passing when we left our home to make our way across the world. It was our first trip, our first time on a plane, without Richard.

We had to have special clothing for the ashram. Women must be covered from head to toe and scarves are worn to cover the shoulders and chest. A few weeks earlier we had gone to Berkeley to pick our punjabis, which are long, colorful embroidered tunics worn over loose fitting pants. It made the girls laugh when they imagined how funny it would be to show up in school wearing their new attire. That night we ate Indian food to introduce them to some of the spices, textures, and tastes; there was a spirit of adventure and preparation for a journey that we were going on together.

Over dinner we talked again about how India held our spiritual roots. They knew that Sai Baba had been one of our most inspiring teachers. Jazz, especially, had been eager to visit his ashram since she was a girl, imagining it like a child imagines a castle in a fairy tale. On the way over, I realized that this was a pilgrimage, like the ones in the stories I'd read to my girls years before. What we were to gain from this voyage was as much about leaving and making our way safely back home on our own as anything else. This trip represented our first steps as a new family unit. While it terrified me to move forward, it was necessary for me to show leadership to my daughters and for them to see we would be safe and capable even if their dad was not with us. In that small way I gained some sense of personal power to take charge of life at a time when everything felt out of control.

We arrived in Bangalore by way of Frankfurt. As we stepped off the tarmac and made our way through customs to pick up our luggage, it was hard to grasp that it was actually two o'clock in the morning.

We walked down a carpet through a roped-off aisle and were assaulted by the sultry heat and the aroma of India; there was a mixture of rich spices, sweat, car exhaust, and sweet flowers. The air was thick and everywhere men stared and raised their arms to get our attention, all wanting to assist with our luggage. I stood in front of the herd like a mama bear, waving them off with a polite shake of my head that said, "No, thank you." When that didn't work and they continued to approach us aggressively, I looked at them in a way that said, "Don't mess with me," and with a pitched voice that even startled me, I switched to one word: "No!"

The chaos and disorder frightened the girls. Cars were parked with no order at all. People seemed to be everywhere, pushed up against each other like sardines. A man grabbed our bags and just started walking at a fast pace to his car while I began chasing after him. A look of panic crossed Jazz's face as she saw me disappear around a corner. I pulled on my bag and took it back from him, and we navigated our way to a taxi line. It had been a rocky start.

We arrived at a beautiful hotel called Leelah Palace, where we would refresh ourselves for a day before moving to the ashram. The contrast between the two locations was marked; the ashram would have only basic necessities and no accoutrements.

Our trip to India mirrored much of the chaos and disorder of the past few months as we navigated from the stability of our previous life to this new, unfolding one. In India, where people see eternity in the earth and where many live with only the necessities of existence, it was not lost on me that the girls would see how some people endure loss every day. Where survival is tougher and life is not easy for the people, it would also make the girls' loss, I hoped, feel less isolating. Wisdom often comes from distant places. At a time when we were shifted wildly between emotional extremes, I hoped that India would help us to live more in the center, to find peace in presence and joy, even amidst the chaos of grief.

Though I had been young, my first trip to India with Richard had made a lasting impression on me. During my marriage I had eased into traditional family routines and I was struck often by the cultural contrasts between what had inspired me then and the life I had slipped into, with its comforts and dangers, in middle-class contentment. Ours was a marriage that had worked like a crystal in a clock. It was so easy to assume that life would just remain the same, that we would find all the answers to our questions and control our destiny. We assumed our health was good because we had made good choices for a healthy lifestyle, or so we fooled ourselves into believing. All illusions, I saw clearly now.

India, too, was an example of contrasts: order amid chaos, and great wealth amid poverty. Yet there were few illusions in the fixed simplicity of life here, bathed in eternities of family and spiritual values that are in such sharp contrast to America, where we have so much materially and so little spiritually.

We hired a car for our journey to the countryside. We began to make our way through the city traffic but quickly came to a stop. We made quite a picture: four fair-haired Western women and our driver. There are no real traffic lanes even in the city, and the cars are just inches from each other. When a traffic signal at last changed, we started moving again, and before long we were beyond the city limits. Small villages came into view, alive in their morning routine. Eighteen years before, Richard and I had taken a drive just like this one, and it seemed that little had changed. I knew he would be pleased that I had brought our girls here. They were fascinated by the culture. It was like stepping back in time for them to see these villages with their Hindu statues, pandits dressed in orange, and women dressed in saris carrying bushels on their heads, their children in tow.

At one point, our driver suddenly pulled off to the side of the road. Our car had a flat tire. We laughed as we had to empty the trunk of our suitcases to help the driver get the spare and to lighten the body of the car so he could crank it up to replace the tire. We had dressed in our Indian clothes of long tunics over pants and scarves, so that we would be ready to enter the ashram. We had to relieve ourselves, and these clothes were not the easiest to negotiate as we stepped off the red clay road and behind a grove of banyan trees. We worried that the driver, who'd already been paid, might not be there when we returned, so Naomi remained with him. As we all finished our business, we walked back up to the road. Standing there was a group of schoolboys, all dressed in uniform, staring with wide eyes as the three blonde Western women appeared, like a vision arriving from nowhere. We were happy to see the tire was changed. We would have a ride to the ashram after all. We commented about how we were given our first lesson in *Trust*.

We entered the ashram gates and observed small signs bearing friendly codes of conduct with Baba's teachings posted in pastel colors. Named Prasanthi Nillyam, Abode of Peace, this was a world all its own we were entering. We were ushered in, along with many hundreds of other devotees, to await the guru's arrival. The first darshan is always exciting. Darshan is simply a visit of blessings from the guru, when he comes out to talk and gaze among the devotees. It is one of two he gives daily. We waited in a mandir, which is a large, covered outdoor auditorium. It was ornately decorated with Hindu statues of Ganesh, Shiva, Krishna, Vishnu, Brahman, and others in pastel colors adorned in gold. The girls had heard stories of Baba before, but as they quietly sat cross-legged, their eyes bright and looking around at the intricate detail of the art in anticipation of his arrival, they could feel the energy of the place. Jazz whispered, "I've been here. I know this place."

I knew then that I was right to trust my intuition to come here. It made me happy that despite the 105-degree heat and rustic accommodations, we had made the long trek. Richard and I were not much older than the girls when we first came here. As a couple, we had traveled a thousand light-years together. Coming here now with our daughters completed the circle.

Over the next few days we settled into a routine. Ashram is a spiritual place of study and spiritual practice. It is neat, orderly, and quiet as each person there is encouraged to create stillness within. It amazed the girls how simple life could be. Our rooms were side-by-side and contained one bathroom, a small kitchen, and a ceiling fan. There was no air conditioning. I thought how proud Richard would be that the girls didn't complain much and sat for hours on the hard cement floor, legs crossed; their water bottles, cell phones, and iPods out of sight, they sat in silent meditation.

Many miracles surround Sai Baba, and he is known to ignite in his devotees a powerful manifestation of spirit. By the time we were ready to leave, I believe the girls understood that their father was present in their lives, even now, and they would always be able to access him through love. I, too, understood the formless in a much deeper way now. Seeing our teacher at this time held comfort for me, but I felt that relationship shifting with the loss of my husband. I had united with Richard in the divine and no longer felt I needed as much from Sai Baba. My path was clearly to detach from all form now, and that might even mean emancipation from my beloved guru for a time. Baba always said, "Don't make it about worshipping me. I am only an example of what you are. The difference between you and me is only that you don't know you are divine." He had taught that we should not worship the form of God but rather worship the source where we are all one, and for the first time I really got this.

Travel has a way of taking you out of where you are emotionally for a brief time so you can view life differently. Making our way across the world and back home again showed us that, with time, we were going to be fine and that everything – everything – flowed from divine grace and order.

One week can sometimes feel like a lifetime and certainly that was how it felt as we returned home. As I entered our house, back in California, I was not prepared for the feeling of despair that overwhelmed me, much like the hot Indian air in Bangalore. I had gone to a sacred place and had felt Richard in that divine space. But now the house was eerily quiet. Was this it? Was that all? I thought as I began to unpack. *Surrender, trust, and accept,* I told myself, as I had done over and again, during the week. He is *gone.* And so, my surrender deepened, as did my faith that I could trust in the outcome, whatever it would be, as I really began to embrace "alone."

10.

THE THINGS PEOPLE SAY

Grief healing happens in a quiet time behind closed doors. Much of the time I was content to stay in the cocoon of my home. I could be with my feelings. Early on, when Richard's presence was so strong there, I had a difficult time leaving. There were reminders all over the house that, just weeks ago, he was still here. I couldn't pull myself away. I also knew not to minimize this tragedy or to try to set it aside in a little corner, neatly packaged. And I understood that when people said, "It's all going to be okay and you'll see that soon," what they really meant was they hoped it would soon be better for *them*. I came to see that people can't look too long at grief; that its untidy, ungovernable side creates awkwardness.

Inevitably, I wanted to go out into the world again – I wanted to, and I had to. There was grocery shopping to do. I arranged to meet friends for coffee or a walk. Eventually, I emerged from my protective cocoon for longer and longer stretches. The girls needed things; there were school events and soccer games to attend. I needed time to get away from grief, to enjoy the pleasure of ordinary activity and simple conversation with community neighbors and shopkeepers. It was time to feel the sun burn through the blue air.

But stepping out again in public was complicated. I have always been positive and upbeat. Whenever I went out, I put a smile on my face; I was unfailingly polite. But now I didn't feel like the same person. I wasn't confident or secure. In the back of my mind, I was always thinking about how Richard wouldn't be there when I got home. People outside, of course, never saw the landmine that was now my life at home. After a loss like this happens, you're not the person you were anymore. You're a new person and you don't know who that is yet. But of course, everybody knew my story.

That made me stand up very quickly. I wanted to appear strong so as to honor Richard. There are people who go through life and no matter what happens to them, no matter how hard they are knocked down, they get back up. I struggled to do that. I knew that wherever I went people looked at me strangely and wondered, how does she do it? How does she smile? I knew I didn't appear to be the grieving widow in the traditional sense. I was young. I was healthy. I was fortunate. Every day I remembered how much God loved us. I told myself, "See all the angels he has sent to care for us." I knew we had been provided for, materially and emotionally. There was abundance in our lives, even in loss. I knew that I was loved and held.

That was what I told myself on my better days. But when you are on your own, every part of your life changes. It's like a big family puzzle where each of you represents a piece that is interwoven. You need each person to complete the puzzle – so when there is a missing piece, there is a hole. The very public fact of Richard's death eased some of the discomfort of going out again. I never had to explain, and there was always support.

But it was very lonely, too.

We had had such a beautiful life, Richard and I, and we had created it together. The end of it was shocking to everybody. Our whole identity as a family crashed. To those outside, our marriage and family had been a source of envy. Now the girls were the ones whose father had died; I was the woman alone. All of a sudden, Richard died and now we had become what everyone dreads.

People want to be kind, but they see you differently. People want to say the right thing, but they don't always have the words. It tested my patience when people pretended they understood what I was feeling. How could they? Empathy stretched only as far as Grief's front yard.

The backyard was where all the pain was. Unfortunately, our cultural response to death is to smooth everything over as fast as possible with dime store sentiments and to simply pretend away anything that might cause pain or discomfort to linger too long. There were times I came to see those who sought to console me through my bloodshot eyes. I was weary and tense. I was raw, and sometimes, I said things I later regretted. I discovered there is no single right way to support others through loss. We walk toward one another under a dark sky across a bridge without handrails. There were missteps, as I describe below, but each encounter showed me something that brought me back to daylight. Experience pulsates with learning.

ENCOUNTER ONE: *The too earnest "How are you, really?"*

I was just coming out of my deepest grief. I was starting to move from protective one-on-one encounters into social engagements around small groups, something I had been completely at ease with before Richard died. I was trying to return to my old self – which I now know is an impossibility.

It was Friday night and a girlfriend was celebrating her fortieth birthday. I didn't know very many of her friends, and therefore counted on finding solace in the anonymity. I sat down at a side table with a glass of wine and a plate of food. A woman I had met at the buffet approached me with that look on her face I had grown to recognize. I winced. *Here we go again,* I thought.

She tilted her head and searched me with sad eyes. She sat a little too near and placed a hand on my shoulder. She was a stranger who felt comfortable enough to ask for the inside story and to impart a little advice, too.

There were many times over the last months when strangers had approached me as innocent well-wishers, who said simply that they hoped that we were doing well and then left me alone. Richard had been a celebrity, and so we had been accustomed to people stopping by our table in restaurants, to being stopped on the street, and, when we traveled, by his readers or by those who simply knew who he was. They liked to ask him questions, to tell their stories. It never bothered Richard because people were always respectful. They didn't pry. They were happy just to shake his hand.

But it had been several months since I had lived that life. This woman with her hand on my shoulder didn't know it, but her intrusion filled me with resentment. My grief was not public domain. At that moment, expressing herself might have been a need that she had, but it was not a need that I had.

I watched as she pulled up a chair and leaned in close. "How *are* you?" she asked.

I responded with a half-smile, "Well, I'm at a party so I must be doing okay." I hoped it would stop right there, that she would pick up on my cue that I didn't want to talk about it. But this woman, whom I had known for five minutes, just nodded and then touched my arm with a familiarity she had not earned. "No, how are you, *really?*"

I was annoyed, really annoyed now, that she expected me to go into my story at a time when I just wanted to be like everyone else at the party. I lost interest in my plate of pasta and put down my fork and napkin. I responded flatly, "Well, every day I wake up and I basically put my feet over my bed and I go from there. I check in to see how I am feeling today."

She stared at me intently and then she offered her advice: "Well, maybe you should think of doing something more with your life." I gave her a long look as my rage at her presumption boiled. I could have taken a deep breath and just nodded. I could have shared my plans, because yes, I had started to make them. There had already been our India trip, and over the next months there would be more travel; there would also be a new book. But I was angry now and needed to speak out for all the times I felt frustrated in this situation.

So I asked her, "Did you come here with your spouse or significant other?" She pointed in his direction. I continued, "Oh, you mean he's alive? Have you ever lost anyone? Has anyone you've been really close to ever died?

"No, actually, well, yes, my grandmother," she replied.

"Okay. Have you ever been through the pain of natural childbirth?"

"No." She looked at me uncertainly. I could tell she was starting to sense my irritation.

"So, you're sitting here telling me that I should do something more with my life when it's less than a year since I lost the person most important to me in that life – something you can't have a clue about because it's never happened to you." I lowered my voice so she would have to lean in to hear me. "Sometimes when I wake up in the morning I feel like an animal that's been skinned and gutted. That's what grief feels like. Please don't profess to tell somebody who's going through that process and who is that raw what to do with their life."

I knew immediately that I had been too harsh. I felt bad. This was probably a nice woman whose intention had been pure. She had taken my wrath on the chin. But oh, it felt good to experience the empowerment of honest expression and the authenticity of feeling that emerges from the grief process. I vowed to remember that, and to set clear boundaries for what I would or would not reveal about myself in the future. Next time, I would remember not to be too harsh. Most people, after all, are trying to be kind. For me, fewer words are better – on both ends.

ENCOUNTER TWO: *"He's in a better place."*

It took me many months to make my way to our local Safeway, the supermarket where Richard and I had shopped for two decades. I had been deliberately going to stores that were smaller or out of the way, where I could slip in and out without running into anyone

I knew. It was three months before I was ready to face the broad community. I saw a very subtle thing happening in the interchange between their expression of comfort and my response. It was as though they were asking me to comfort them in *their* grief for Richard and to allay their concern for the three of us. If I made it to the grocery store, I really didn't feel like having a pity party in the fruit aisle with whomever I had run into. Small errands gave me a chance to change my context, to lighten the burden of grief in the smallest of ways. I just wanted to do something normal, one thing from my old life.

I noticed that when I bumped into someone for the first time since Richard's death, there was almost always a moment that felt like an instant replay. Whoever it was inevitably looked at me with a mixture of uneasiness (*"Uh-oh-it's her! The Widow Carlson"*) and shock (*"What do I say to her?"*), then held her breath, and welled up with tears while I, too, took a deep breath and braced myself for the words. I learned to smile and wave and mouth the words. "We're doing okay. The girls are all right and I am fine." Invariably, people would tell me stories about where they were when they heard the news and how shocked they had been. As the details of their stories washed over me, reminding me and upsetting me once again, I thought to myself, Yeah, you think *you* were surprised? What was worse was hearing people say, "You know he's in a better place." I would fight back the temptation to say what was in my heart: "He may well be, but that is little comfort to us right now." And, somehow, I knew, even as Richard may well be in bliss, he would have wanted to stay right alongside his family; there was still so much life to live.

Before Richard died, I, too, must have said some ridiculous things to grieving people. The right words are hard to find. Losing Richard taught me that some moments just require a hug and no words at all.

ENCOUNTER THREE: *"I'm sorry for your loss."*

The things people say to fill the awkwardness of that first encounter often come off as more trite than heartfelt. "I'm sorry for your loss" may perhaps be the emptiest expression of bereavement ever. "Loss?" I want to scream, "I didn't lose him. He's gone." Richard was not misplaced, somewhere to be found. You don't "lose" your husband! Nor did the word "loss" begin to describe the annihilation of the life my daughters and I once knew.

Three weeks before he died, Richard wrote the foreword to a friend's book. When publication time came, I wanted to represent Richard at the launch, as I knew this was a place he would be standing if he were still alive. I also used to love parties, but when I entered the room, for the first time in my life, I felt shy. In that room of smiling faces, I felt like an elephant on display. I loathed grieving publicly. I was extremely sensitive to energy and noise. "Face your fear," I heard my own voice say. "Own it. Don't be afraid." That was hard to do when I knew that as soon as people learned I was Richard Carlson's widow, they would come and ask me how I was doing.

Sure enough, a man approached and introduced himself. As he shook my hand, he said, "I'm sorry for your loss." He followed with, "You have to be grateful that you experienced such an amazing relationship. Most people will never be able to say that."

All I wanted to say to him was, "Fuck you." It surprised me that sympathy could be a trigger for anger. But his words sounded empty and condescending. I wondered why people could think it was so simple to move on so easily after loss.

I responded instead by explaining that Richard was not lost like a set of car keys, but thanked him anyway. I look back now and again regret that I was ungracious. In reality, there really is little anyone can say. Few words offer much good and many words can become annoying, especially words that convey the suggestion of how someone is supposed to be in their grief. Telling someone how to be in their grief is one of the worst things anyone can do. What I wanted to say back to people was this: "Tell me you pray for me that I will have strength and will find my way with God's hand holding mine, but don't assume I need your pity. That does nothing for me."

The people who told me how to be in grief, who presumed to know what they could not possibly understand, nonetheless helped me, however unintentionally. They allowed me to access my anger. Anger is a vital expression of grief. I am grateful to all those who patiently endured my expressions of grief through anger and who responded with compassion even as I rejected, sometimes rather rudely, their attempts to console me.

ENCOUNTER FOUR: *People who feed off drama and thrive on tragedy.*

For me, grief was a constant struggle between needing to stay present in it and resisting the pull of getting stuck in my "story." If pity angered me, self-pity frightened me – getting stuck in it would destroy any chance I had to make a new life.

Somehow, everyone wanted to "share" their stories of loss or stories they had heard about. Usually I listened with compassion and interest, but one story in particular showed me how careful I needed to be. When I called to make an appointment to get my washing machine repaired, the woman on the phone told me about how she had lost her husband five years earlier. She told me the story of his death as if it had happened yesterday, and I heard her agonized self-pity. That was a future I did not want. Wow, I thought, this woman is locked in her story. She will be a widow for a very long time." She had completely identified with her tragedy.

It was an important moment for me, as I saw her as an example of someone I did not want to become. This is what excessive grief looked like. For her, it was far from over. I saw how easy it would be to fall victim to my "story," to become obsessed by its illogic and unfairness and how, if I allowed it, I could feel sorry for myself for a very long time. I did not want to become the Victim of what had happened to us – lost to the past and lost in the possibilities of a future we would not share. I wanted to move forward, no matter how slow or painful that might be.

ENCOUNTER FIVE: *Saying nothing at all.*

You can always tell someone who has experienced "loss" over someone whose losses are still on the horizon by the way they respond to yours. I bumped into an acquaintance, the mother of my daughter's friend, as she pulled her car into the parking space outside our local drugstore. She stepped out as she saw me, and waited for a sign that I wanted contact. I motioned to her and she slowly walked up and removed her sunglasses so that I could see the compassion in her eyes. Her hands reached up to hold my shoulders. In an unusually intimate move, she lifted her face close to mine and she looked into my pain, unafraid of what she would find there. Her tears matched mine and she said, "Kris, there are no words I have for you. Just know my heart is with you as I think of you and the girls every day." That was all the comfort I needed. Those few words were the truest expression of condolence I had received. They felt right for me.

The people who best understand what you are going through are those who have known loss themselves. We all come to discover this uncharted territory sooner or later. We will lose parents, and a few of us will endure losses that are unimaginable with cruel timing. Pain and loss are inseparable. The acknowledgement of the pain, and the assurance that you are being supported with thoughts and prayers is all anyone needs to know.

When people don't know what to say, that is the best thing to say.

Anything else is trite up against the raw openness of the person who is grieving.

ENCOUNTER SIX: *"Keep busy."*

Perhaps more common than drugs and alcohol as a means of numbing pain is distraction. Many people said to me, "It's good for you and the girls to keep busy."

I would want to say, "No, it's really not. You just don't understand because you've never dealt with pain any other way."

I learned after being cracked wide open that society wants to hide pain; society wants us to stay busy and cover it up. But it messes you up to stay busy. You have feelings that surface unpredictably in your grief. You have to move with them, like trees do when they bend with a stiff wind. Resistance will snap you. You also need to respect that you have a different life to live right now. Being busy interrupts and trivializes that process of healing – as though you can't trust the truth that, eventually, you will heal. You will come back.

As I learned to trust my own responses to what people said, elegant or clumsy, I knew they were all, in their way, trying to lift me up. I came to understand that the right words gave me permission to let go. In this new life I had to let go of an idea. We were not the family to be envied anymore. I could see that in people's eyes. I wasn't the person I had been anymore. We were a family in crisis. I had to let go of everything. It takes a lot of trust to let go, and words of comfort helped me find the confidence to do that. The right words catch us when we are falling and the wrong words crack us open a little more to relieve the building pressure of our wounds.

Grief opened me to more honest expression than I was used to in my previous life. As I passed through the most difficult part of my process, I learned how to speak my mind in ways that were respectful but more honest. I became better at telling people how I felt, what I wanted, and what I *didn't* want them to say.

I now understand that there is a divine force in all of us that drives us to reach out and comfort those in pain, as best as we are able. I have learned that when we do so, we stumble our way to a deeper, more tuned-in sense of compassion for one another.

11.

FOLLOW YOUR FEAR

In the beginning of my grief, every choice I made was the result of answering one of two questions: What would Richard do if he were here? And, What am I most afraid of doing without him?

During my first hours of life without him, I sat in the same leather chair I had sat in many times before while discussing life with Richard, and I knew I faced a fork. One path would be of tremendous growth and would honor my own presence on this earth. The other was a long corridor of darkness and depression. I had no real choice.

Even though I didn't know how I would possibly get through a life without him, I vowed my love to him and promised I would honor Richard by creating purpose in my own life.

I knew I had to step into the fire. In order to move *through* it I had to start by moving *into* it. Eventually, I would come to realize that, more than anything, "it" was my fear.

There had been moments over the previous months when I had been tempted by ugly fantasies. Some of that was fueled by "why us?" anger at God when I would rage, "Out of all the people in the world for this to happen to, why would it happen to Richard?" I sometimes saw myself buried under the covers with greasy, unkempt hair and dark circles under squinting eyes that peered belligerently at whomever was opening the blinds to let in the light and shake me from sorrow. That was when I allowed self-pity to sink its teeth into my already-tender skin.

Thankfully, that never lasted very long. I got up. But for a time, the simple lockstep of "Eat Sleep Breathe" was my singular focus. Every other decision I made in the moment, each and every moment, with an eye to just getting through alive.

And then that passed, too. By midwinter and spring, I wanted out of the rumpled bed of the worst of my imagination. I wanted to feel Life again in my bloodstream. Still, I was scared. When you are vulnerable and you feel you have lost so much, everything seems risky. You don't want to lose what little you still have, and fear shows you, like nothing else, just what it is you value. But I learned that nothing pulls the sorrow out of you, especially if your sorrow is tinged with self-pity, better than following your fear, because it feeds your courage to continue on at a time when everything is baby steps taken on shaking legs.

Before Richard died, one of his favorite office assistants from a few years earlier had become engaged. Nicole had planned to ask Richard to officiate at the wedding and was devastated by his death. During a phone conversation one morning, she told me there was something she wanted to ask me. When I realized the purpose of her call, I drew in my breath. Nicole had been sad, trying to think of who would replace Richard at the upcoming event when it suddenly occurred to her: She wanted *me*.

I remembered a time many years before when I had talked Richard into officiating at a wedding. He said later that it had been among the most stressful things he had ever done. I was already feeling anxious about attending my first wedding, not as a wife, but as a widow. A grip of fear knotted my belly; immediately, I said, "Yes! I'll do it!"

I wanted to help Nicole, but there was another reason for me to agree to her request. It would begin to prepare me for the fall, when I would bring my grief forward, in a very public way, with the publication of Richard's final book.

An Hour to Live, an Hour to Love was something private, a letter he wrote for me on the occasion of our eighteenth wedding anniversary, three years before he passed. Richard had been inspired to answer the questions posed by Stephen Levine: "If you had one hour to live, who would you call, what would you say, and why are you waiting?" Richard gave me his "response," tied up with a gold ribbon, at Sea Ranch, our house on the Mendocino Coast.

I read it while sitting on our favorite bench looking out to the Pacific, moved by the sunset against a brilliantly streaked sky. Tears ran down my face while I read. I wondered what could have possibly motivated him to do this. I looked up and asked Richard if there was health news he wasn't telling me. Even for Richard, this was an astounding letter. He looked at me with an expression of pure love and told me that no matter what happened to us in the rest of our lives, he didn't want to wait to say the things that burst in his heart for me every day.

After Richard died, I searched his computers and shelves looking for the document. It had been years since he had given it to me, but he had gone back and added to it, and edited it for publication. Then he put it away. Four weeks after he died, I found the file, and read it. It seemed so very clear to me that by publishing it, I would honor Richard's life so that his readers around the world could know something very special about the man beyond the books that touched their hearts.

I wanted Richard's life and work to carry on. By bringing this book to the public, I believed I could maintain his space in the world. It would be an act of continuation, like creating a scholarship or a foundation can be, or planting a tree or a rosebush for a departed loved one – all ways to signal that those left behind are moving *forward* without moving on. Publishing *An Hour to Live, An Hour to Love* would be the tree I planted for Richard – my gift to honor my life with him and to show the world the lovely man he truly was.

That March, Richard's publisher took the book enthusiastically, but to launch it correctly during its planned publication in December, I would be required to promote it. Public speaking and book tours never unsettled me when Richard was by my side, but the prospect of speaking about him, without him, frightened me. The opportunity

Nicole was offering me came into my path at the right moment. I knew this would prepare me for something ahead that was going to be hard for me to do. What better way to confront my fear and sadness than by participating so visibly at an occasion that recognized the beginning of a married life, at a time when I was facing the end of mine.

Fear is something I have grown accustomed to recognize when I am moving into a new direction – a direction closer to my authentic self. Living completely alive means moving *into* and *through* discomfort and noticing the fears that can otherwise hide in our unconscious choices. I noticed my fears with greater intensity as my life slowed and I was alert and "lived presently" after Richard died. One of the gifts grief gave me was the clarity to see that following my fear would heal me at a deeper level. Fear became a guide to freedom – the freedom to be me.

Preparing for the wedding was a big leap into the fire. These preparations happened to coincide with all those "firsts" without Richard. This proved to be the most difficult time of my grief – Mother's Day. Richard's birthday, Jasmine's prom, graduation, and Father's Day were all ahead. Each special occasion had the potential to deliver a thunderbolt that would drive home our longing for husband and father, and attempt to steal our moments of celebration like a thief in the night.

I was still raw and dreaded reviewing the details of the marriage service. I waited as long as I could to memorize the note cards I had marked and color-coded. Every time I sat down to work, the undertow of memory would pull and tug at me and I would sob. It was a battle to stay focused and not to feel sorry for myself. This moment belonged to Nicole and her fiancé, Jim - their dreams, their vision. But when I did allow myself a moment to reflect, I thought of my own marriage that ended suddenly with dreams yet to be completely filled, I shook my head. What had it all been about? It suddenly occurred to me we were so busy living life that we had never even looked at our wedding videotape together.

It was difficult in the beginning for me to look at all our books in the *Don't Sweat the Small Stuff* brand, and especially the ones we worked closely on together. This was another hoop of fear to face and move through – carrying on for Richard. I asked Nicole and Jim to read *Don't Sweat the Small Stuff in Love* and come to my house for dinner to discuss their favorite chapters as a sort of premarital counseling. That's what we four would have done together. Instead, Jim, Nicole and I sat on the couch in our living room. They spoke about their dreams and what they wanted from marriage, and we used the chapters they chose like a trampoline to then discuss other issues and concerns they had about relationships and marriage. I shared with them the best parts about ours.

I recalled a discussion we had about relationships when we were figuring out the order of our chapters in *Don't Sweat the Small Stuff in Love* and we chose "Mostly Be Pals" as the one to start the book. We often laughed about how every couple should write a book about relationships together and save themselves years of marriage counseling. We hoped couples would use our book to facilitate better communication and deepen their connection by realizing the power of their love. Writing it together certainly solidified the power of ours. We had determined that the three most important things to care for every day and take notice of in marriage were friendship, respect, and appreciation; shared values; and dreams. When a marriage is grounded in that kind of mutuality, everything else just follows in a natural ebb and flow like the tides and the seasons.

The day of the ceremony finally came. As I stood before the one hundred guests waiting for the ceremony to begin, I was prepared but nervous and unsure if I would be able to remain composed throughout the forty-five-minute ceremony. It was a garden wedding. There was a fountain behind us. I pressed the backs of my legs against the fountain's cool edge to stop the shaking of my knees, closed my eyes, and breathed deeply. I then looked around me as the late afternoon sun sprayed the garden in straw-colored light. The scent of lemon and roses was palpable. I smiled at the vibrant couple's friends and families.

After the ceremony I walked deeper into the gardens, sat on a hidden bench for some privacy, and looked up into the blue skies. There was a sweeping army of angels in the clouds, long brushstrokes of them, undeniably Richard. I reached high to the sky in an attempt to gather him into me and cried quietly for the years we had and the years ahead.

When I agreed to officiate at Nicole's wedding, I was deep in. Yet I knew that doing something that was both public and intimate would help me come into my Self, and stand on new legs. That day proved to me how strong I am, but also how deeply I loved and honored the commitment of marriage. It delivered me to a full circle where I could evaluate and be grateful for my own.

Fear is a clear and unmistakable guide toward our highest, most powerful self. All we had to do was lean in.

If I wanted to honor my beloved in the way I lived life, I had to first choose to live it *all the way*. I ask the question often: What are you most afraid of? Whatever the answer, that is where you need to be. Follow your fear, face it, and find love.

12.

EVERYONE'S SISTER

I am too young to be a widow. One afternoon my girlfriend and I were sitting around and talking. We stared into each other's tear-filled eyes as I moaned, "I'm a widow now." Then we simultaneously burst out laughing as the image "widow" conjured itself in juxtaposition to me. We decided that there should be a new name for forty-something women whose husbands pass in midlife, something like "willow."

I instantly became everyone's sister. As women, we take care of each other like sisters when our marriages end in divorce, when we have sick children or are sick ourselves, and when any number of tragedies befall us. Women reflexively rally to support women, and for many, it's okay for men to care for close female friends, too. "Sister" is a sacred and safe frame for both men and women.

In the beginning, Richard's closest friends, many of whom were my girlfriends' husbands, banded around to protect us from the outside world like a firewall. I found it fascinating that these instincts are innate and that death wakes us, each in our own way, to meet in our grief. There was a deep need among his friends to let me know they were watching out for me and my daughters, and that I was not without male influence. Yet, I missed my man and the intimacy that we shared every day.

I didn't have many male relationships outside of my marriage. All of my energy went to Richard and the kids, to my girlfriends, and to our parents, teachers, and soccer family relationships. But I immediately missed the maleness of Richard's presence, of just having that male perspective to balance and center all the feminine energies of our home.

Richard had a wonderful way of disarming all the emotional "drama" by his grounding presence and peaceful perspective.

We lived in a couples' world that revolved around family life. Now it felt odd to hang out with my friends who were still partnered and married. The awkwardness did not come from them but from me. I did not feel comfortable with growing too close in my friendships with my girlfriends' husbands as I quickly felt a new, subtle barrier of being a woman on my own. I didn't feel comfortable at dinner parties where odd-numbered seats at the table made me self-conscious. I turned down many invitations. The weekends could be long. The girls were busy, and I didn't want them to feel responsible for me. They needed to be with their friends and try to be in their lives as normally as the circumstances allowed. I came to dread Friday and Saturday nights. Sunday mornings, too, reminded me I was no longer coupled.

You don't ever count on being a widow at forty-three. You're not young any longer, but the fountain has not stopped flowing – that's for darned sure. We know that women enter the prime of their sexual lives in their forties. Still, I never would have anticipated that my libido would explode shortly after Richard died. I found myself in the throes of a most bewildering hormonal hurrah that was brought on by post-traumatic stress and a very powerful spiritual awakening.

When Richard and I were raising our babies, and in that incredible physical exhaustion phase, our sex life was something of an effort. Richard often awoke early, and I mean really early, to write. His day job was counseling people; I stayed home with the girls. We fell into bed at night after the nighttime routine and we were asleep in seconds. Still, busy as we were, we made it a point to schedule "date nights." It was important to stay connected, and we needed to have our own playtime. One summer evening as we were on our way to our usual dinner and a movie, we passed a local Marriott Hotel. We looked at each other longingly and Richard said, "C'mon, let's have some fun."

He made a sharp turn into the parking lot. We ditched our original plan for several hours of spontaneous, spectacular intimacy.

Richard used to joke around with me and say, "I can't wait till you get into that forty-something phase, Kris," thinking how happy he'd be when I wanted sex all the time. It was too ironic that I had arrived in this totally wanton state without him.

I was having an especially rough night just eight weeks into my mourning, on February 13. It would be my very first Valentine's Day without Richard. I was anxious and lonely. Oh, God, I thought. How can I do this? How do I get through another day? It's Valentine's Day tomorrow! What about sex? Oh my God, what do I do about sex? My thoughts were surging without order, and I remember thinking about it, feeling a bit ashamed later that I had even considered sex at all.

Physical passion was a part of my life I took for granted. When you are in a loving marriage where true intimacy is as much about your emotional and intellectual connection as your physical, then your sex life adds a deeper connection as an expression of your love. Richard and I were so connected that way. It was like we were one body. It was hard to even picture myself with another man after a quarter century of devotion to Richard. I confided to a spiritual friend, "Why have I been so turned on sexually since Richard died?" And she told me that the divine energy that opens up in us when we are awakened at such a deep level, as grief will do, feels eerily similar to sexual arousal. Well, I thought, I was single and celibate, but unwilling to explore the theory further. I just hoped that I would not do something really out of character and throw myself in loneliness at some random individual of the male gender.

But then something unexpected happened.

Early on, a distant acquaintance of Richard's reached out and offered support. The doorbell rang and there was a lovely spring bouquet with a card that read: "Kris, Jazzy, and Kenna: Richard was a great man and a dear friend. I am deeply saddened for your loss." I was touched by this man's thoughtfulness. Richard had spoken of him over the years and had admired him very much. I had always wanted to meet this man, and now as I wrote a thank-you note, I secretly hoped we would become friends. His reply offered just that. We began a parallel healing journey through our respective grief; as it turned out, he was also suffering through a difficult breakup with a woman he loved very deeply. From my home in the Bay Area and an ocean away, we began to know one another. The understanding between us was immediate and entire. His friendship dangled me a rope that helped me surface from a very deep hole of loneliness and longing for Richard that his absence had thrown me into. After several months of e-mail correspondence and telephone conversations that felt very much like soul brother and sister, we decided to meet in person for dinner.

I was surprised by our chemistry. After many hours of talking and enjoying each other's company, I said, "It's late now, you have to work tomorrow and I have a meeting scheduled. I think I'll go to my room now." He asked me quietly, "Do you really want to leave?" I looked at him like a deer in headlights as my heart began to pound and I felt heat rise to my cheeks.

"Are you suggesting what I think you are?" I asked. "I'm not sure I am ready for that."

In a very gentle and low tone he said, "We can take it very slow, Kris, and stop at any time if you feel uncomfortable. I would just like to kiss you."

As he lowered his head, I ducked to the side. "I need water," I said. It was as if I was a virgin, or worse, about to have my very first kiss – ever. I gulped the water down, patted my lips, and turned to make sure this was a real-time step I was ready to take.

I decided to take a bath. As I watched the water fill the tub, the words rang: "Until death do you part." Was it too soon for this? But who could tell me when was too soon, or when it would be right? I was curious and afraid; there was my drumming, numbing fear of being seen and touched by another man. The idea of being intimate with another man had seemed unfathomable just weeks earlier, terrain I could not see myself trekking for a long time. But now I was facing my fears, and at this time, my complicated feelings around dating were at the top of the list. I didn't want to be impulsive. I knew I needed to go inside and check in with myself to be sure this was what I wanted to do. I had been led to this moment and the voice that came out of stillness would not steer me wrong.

Richard and I had been all relationships to each other. We were mother, father, best friends, brother and sister, and lovers. Ours was a fulfilling union in all categories of relationship. With that gone, I had asked myself quite often in private hours when I would awaken in our empty bed, fix myself coffee, and watch the sun rise over Mount Diablo: *Who am I without you?* That was my first question. Five months after his death, I was still asking it. But I realized that Richard would want me to do what I had to do to survive this loss. Male companionship was a physical and emotional need for me, and he would support that. I could imagine him speaking to me, his voice direct and sure, even in death. Let that man hold you. Let that man heal you. Let that man comfort you, *because you have to survive this.*

I trusted this man; I knew he cared for me, and so I decided that I would not regret this decision. I was not thinking about entering into the singles world or dating, and I didn't think that he and I would embark on a serious romantic relationship because of the great distance between us, given our home bases. I also knew I no longer belonged to Richard on a physical plane, even though my spirit would be with him forever. I had to *live.*

We shared the longing in our bodies to be held as we discovered each other physically. And the remarkable thing is that I found that I wasn't lost. By this time, I knew what I needed and had decided to trust that it would come to me and that I would embrace it. Something told me that I needed this right now. I didn't feel like it was wrong and I was free from any kind of guilt. A sexual relationship makes you feel alive. As my wise friend had said, the sexual and divine are intimately and wondrously tied together like a figure eight.

We called our few rendezvous "vacations from grief." We would meet to put all the pain aside and allow ourselves the luxury of reprieve as we laughed, talked, dined, drank champagne, and prepared to heal some more. Most of the time we traveled on parallel journeys and occasionally we connected and shared in person. It helped when we were on our own to know we had the support of each other, independent of our family and other friends. It was a very special friendship that existed in a pool of lamplight where we could be together and share passion and conversation that were unique to our shared moment.

While it started out as Richard's friend holding out a hand to comfort his widow, this gentleman became my friend and healing partner in the months we were connected as we both grieved. He encouraged me to stay in it and allow it to move through me. It was a mutually nourishing connection as we held the space for growth and expansion. He helped me recover a part of myself that was alive and vibrant, something I would need to stay healthy as I continued to travel the path of suffering and to see my daughters through their day-to-day lives. Our connection was intense and something to look forward to, a connection that came to me if for no other reason than to remind me of a passionate way through life, and to show me that I had much to look forward to. The life of love was far from over for me. I knew that I was going to live a beautiful second life.

After several months, he returned to the relationship he grieved. Rekindling that love lost was, of course, not a possibility for me. Eventually, though, I knew I would meet another man who would help bring me back into life and to my next level of healing. Eventually, I added a new coverlet to my bed. It was Indian, like the pillows Richard used to lie across. I slipped the coverlet we had used together beneath it. The old and the new could coexist.

I will always be filled with gratitude for having had this man's male perspective and support as I felt the strength of his step alongside mine during the most difficult passage of my grief.

13.

THE FAMILY DANCE

One of the things I learned raising children is that everything falls apart frequently, and then as a family you pull it all together again. You might have a routine or system in place for a while, and then a new issue appears and you must get creative and form a new strategy. In grief, we lived the same way.

One day our life as a family was pretty darn close to idyllic, and the next day it had been ripped apart by death and separation. At first, we just survived and embraced each other, holding tightly to what we had left. But it was a process, and the seasons led us. That first winter the girls found themselves back in school feeling like their childhood had stopped; they were young birds pushed out of the nest too early, unable to express their emotions freely. They were vulnerable and raw and didn't want to be so fully exposed, but everything, it seemed, exposed them.

There was a terrible loneliness as spring came, as if the lengthening days only served to enhance our emptiness; but now it was summer, a sharp, insistent time, a cache for memory and unexpected beginnings. Fall would come and remind us we were rounding the last curve of an unimaginable year. Each season seduced us with hope as we stepped into the world, searching for solid ground.

For a long time, the day-to-day moments, like just getting to school in one piece, had been big; a day without breaking down in front of classmates was a success. At least that's how Kenna and Jazz felt as they navigated the fishbowl of the remaining school year while feeling stared at, being seen as objects of pity. The community was incredibly supportive, but they were now those pretty girls whose famous father had died.

Returning to school just three weeks after Richard's death, both girls had trouble sleeping and concentrating. They complained that their brains felt fuzzy; memorization was difficult. Physics had been difficult enough for Jazz before this; it now became a serious threat to her qualification for graduation.

I did everything I could to ensure that their schools were in a position to be supportive. I met with their principals and discussed ways that we could lighten their load and take some of the pressure off. I pulled Kenna out of two classes so she could arrive at school later and get more sleep. It was ironic. Richard hadn't wanted her to have such a heavy schedule this year; we had talked about that a lot before the school term started the previous September. Those conversations came back to me now. It was almost as though this time had been coming, and deep down Richard knew it.

Most of Jazz's teachers were extremely supportive, except for one who took a hard line with her, saying things like, "You're going to have to toughen up." and "Learn to power through life." When I asked him to dial down the demands of her workload, he suggested instead the twenty things she should do, additionally, to increase her skills. Even after I did all I could to help my children, I had to accept that there were going to be people in their paths who did not know how to show compassion and were uncomfortable with suffering.

In the beginning, I wanted to just to pull them out of school for a year so they could have the space to grieve fully and heal. School has transformed from something that seeds the mind and develops the skills of our youth to a thing that overwhelms them with competitive pressures, and where creative and spontaneous thoughts are left unnourished by curriculum mandates. I knew that what it takes to survive high school, intellectually and socially, would leave no room for the aftermath of tragedy. But Kenna and Jazz did not want to put school on pause. They feared falling behind, not matriculating with their friends, and were surprised to find a safe structure in the incremental blocks of the school day.

In grief, children have different challenges because their coping skills are immature, and they have to participate with such fervor in their school life. Even when things are going well, there is very little breakwater around the teenage years. Add to that the extreme and sudden disruption Jazz and Kenna faced, and it is understandable that their transition to this new life was slow and fragile.

We were a family in grief, but we were also a household of individuals. Each of us had to be allowed her own way of grieving while also tending to each other – that was challenging at best. Certain days seemed to hold particular pieces of the grief process; one day might be tough for one of us and maybe better for another. I imagined us as participants in a circle dance; one of us would step out of the circle to express what she needed, breaking the circle for a time, after which we dancers would then re-form in a different place. I kept faith that our love and need for one another would bring us back into each other's arms.

Each of the girls struggled. Jazz was depressed for a time. There was a dark and sad look in her eyes I had never seen before. The sweet rewards of senior year – college acceptance, prom, and graduation – were clouted by the sadness her father wasn't there to share them. Kenna's love was soccer, but that winter and spring she stopped playing to her full potential. The world of competitive sports leagues cedes nothing to personal circumstance, and in a political move, she and five others were cut and replaced with players from a rival team. When she was severed from her soccer "family" after seven years of camaraderie, her rage poured out at yet another loss. Her grief was triggered in a whole new way.

Jazz and I rallied in commiseration around Kenna, and we said the word "fuck" a lot that weekend as we raged at the injustice that had happened. In the end she joined a team that had a better record and ended up playing and enjoying herself more than she had been. Later, I could see this situation as an opportunity to release some of her anger and pent up grief emotions. Rather than try to smooth it over, I encouraged her anger and full expression of loss. The timing of this was terrible, though: another emergency adjustment and transition that threw us off our feet. And yet as a family we found our balance and we went on.

People said to me, "You have your girls. They will keep you going." Yes, that was true and I thank God for them. But sometimes I felt that people think having children is a simple, one-sided equation. The point was we had *each other*. And I could no more serve as a substitute for the security of a father's arms and guidance than they could replace the loss of my life partner and best friend. I could not fill the role of a father and they could not fill the role of a husband. It wasn't so simple.

Yet, I can't deny it. My girls have been here for me in ways that clearly saved me, in ways that made me feel shakily inadequate as their mother. At first, I was so lost in that initial tsunami of shock that I was unable to take care of them. Sometimes Kenna would find me on the Pilates Reformer in the exercise room, sobbing and balled into grief, my hands still in the handles. My eyes squeezed shut, I would realize she had her arms wrapped around me and that I was the child in those moments, she the mother. She comforted me as her own tears fell. There were many times when Jazz held both of us, and times when I held them. Grief is so direct; you express what is in you at that moment; fever, fugue, or waltz, we danced as our bodies and emotions told us what to do. We teamed to take care of each other, the girls caring for me as much as I did them. Whatever concept I had of myself before this as a strong, wise, maternal figure took a tumble. It was as difficult for me as it was for them to see me crumble before their eyes.

As that first year wore on, it seemed at times like an unending list of momentous dates to just get through. Each "special" day took on new meaning and held a qualified joy, everything filtered through the prism of Richard's absence. I had read that months four to seven are the hardest grief period to endure, and so they were. Kenna passed her driving test and Jazz was admitted to her first-choice college, the University of Oregon. My excitement was genuine as I took her in my arms for a hug, but she seemed so very sad. "I can't leave you and Kenna," her voice quivered. "I'm not going."

I looked at her and remembered how she had painted the word "senior" on her Mustang at the beginning of the school year and how Richard and I had laughed. What should have ended in celebration now seemed pointless. Jazz had worked so hard to bring her GPA up to increase her options. She graduated with a 4.0 her final semester, and here she was, feeling only fearful about our well-being.

But there was no talking her out of it. We sent in her admissions deposit to a local college, her safe school, and all seemed settled. Then things changed. *Again.* Jazz became involved with a boy she had known from years earlier. When he named a star after her for her birthday, I suspected that things might be somewhat serious between them. I was not, however, prepared for what she was about to ask of me. "Mom," she said, "I need to be with Brennan. I want to move up north with him and I'll enroll in a junior college there." That's right. She went from planning to attend a competitive four-year university, to the safe neighborhood college, to wanting to move four hours away, where she would attend community college while living with her boyfriend. I hadn't even met him yet. Oh my God, I thought. This is Richard's fucking nightmare!

I felt the resistance inside me build. I had to be both the mother and the father in this situation. I saw that for the first time in her life, my natural-born cheerleader was feeling antisocial. Then it occurred to me to try to look and see and feel my way through this idea with her, instead of each of us just reacting from our old, expected positions, because everything was different now. For us both, learning to make decisions from a different place was as important as any part of our transition into our new life. And so, I listened to her heart as she told me she wasn't ready to be in a college environment where everyone would be happy, tightly focused on their studies, and playing hard. She needed quiet time to heal, and I realized that I needed to step outside my own thinking and my fears to support her.

Jazz knew what it was going to take to heal, and after I met Brennan I knew he was the one to support her in her process. He was undeniably gentle, kind, and grounded; there was a peaceful presence to him that reminded me of Richard. Until now, Jazz was so worried about Kenna and me that her own grief was getting buried. I went for a long walk and remembered that night right after Richard died when Berenice had helped bring Richard back to us and what he had said about Jazz, our natural-born nurturer and caretaker. It was true. Jazz had really stepped into her role as the big sister, helping with driving and pitching in as she never had with household chores. *Surrender and trust,* I told myself. She was eighteen now – the same age I was when Richard and I met and fell in love. Now she would explore Love, too, while continuing her education. I would respect her choices. She would know what to do. She would find her way.

Jazz would not be moving up north until August, but already Kenna was devastated by the idea of her older sister's absence. We would go from a household of four to three to two. It was not only another big adjustment, in Kenna's mind it put more pressure on her to support and take care of me in ways that she and Jazz once had shared. It would be a lot of change to endure for a girl who just turned fifteen and had begun to wear her feelings of abandonment on her sleeve. Our circle broke again, and we needed to find a new way to dance back to each other to complete it.

I decided that we needed to change our context – to return to our roots, literally, in order to help us find our shape as a family, as its outline was to bend again. Both Richard's and my family are third-generation Swedish – specifically, from Gothenburg, a port city on that country's west coast. We used to joke about the possibility of our being distantly related cousins. So, when we had received a "Hold the Date" card the previous fall to attend a friend's family celebration in Sweden in July, Richard thought we should plan to go. He said, "I have always wanted to take the girls and show them their heritage." Now the three of us would do that together.

We spent several days in Stockholm, captivated by the city's loveliness and swept up in the extravagance of the formal party. The girls wore ballroom gowns and had a good time sampling champagne. An eight-course meal was followed by an evening of theater entertainment – ballet, orchestral music, and song. All around us were magnificent floral arrangements. Tall topiary rosebushes were adorned with artichokes, with fresh-cut cantaloupes that were heather-mounded at the bases.

By the third day, however, the girls were burned out by the four-hour meals with the older crowd. As young people, they were thinking about what they were missing at home. They questioned me for bringing them on this "fancy" trip. For a moment they ganged up on me. "Our dad dies and first you drag our butts all the way to India and then Sweden? Who does that?" I had to laugh at the sanity of that remark. It was true. But I was also forced to realize how much of a team Richard and I had been. It was the girls – and us. Sitting in this hotel room, I felt singled out and alone. My team player was missing. Single parenting was different and lonely. I thought every day about how I was trying to do my best.

Fortunately, the balance of our holiday was more of an old-fashioned trip. The stresses of the last seven months and the uncertainty of those ahead fell away as we drove between the coasts. The road was flat and open, and every mile opened my senses and attitude. As we cruised by small villages with their bright yellow, red and blue-shuttered, tole-painted farmhouses, I understood that this is why we came to Sweden. I knew it had been hard for the girls to see me in such pain over these long months, for them to see me so vulnerable and child-like. I couldn't erase that. But I felt that in some ways, it had been good for me to expose such raw emotions to them. Though every family must find its equilibrium anew every day, in certain ways our lives had been turned upside down without the routines, habits, and responses we used to fall back on – our comfort of knowing what to expect every day was destroyed. Yet, I noticed that there was a usable advantage to my vulnerability. I was more honest. I was more open to the true closeness. I was, perhaps, a deeper and wiser role model to them than I had ever been. It was good for the girls to see this. I was doing my best to model a healthy way to grieve, hoping that it would give them permission to grieve also.

Over the last months, I had hoped my girls would learn to trust in the integrity of their characters, yet be alert to change. Life will test you, and in the journey, we need kindness, adaptability, preparation, and patience in abundance. It's all about Love, I have told them; love spares us the energy of anger, the waste of denial, and depletion of spirit. Returning to this place from where our family came helped me remind us just how far our family had now come, we three Carlson women – dancing through life together.

The previous fall, Richard and I would always find ourselves in tears whenever we thought of Jazz leaving us. We wanted to relish that final year with her. And now it was time. The month after our return from Sweden found us packing Jazz for her move away. It was funny how that concept had lost much of the sting it once had. Now it felt like just another segment of life's ride. Instead of clinging tightly to old ideas of how things should go, or were supposed to go, according to some vision I dreamed up years ago, I realized I could let go and enjoy. We decided to make an adventure out of the move. We packed up a U-Haul truck with miscellaneous "overflow" of furniture and accessories from my garage, and worked together, in a very short time, to make her first home away from home as comfortable as a well-worn pair of shoes.

That period also coincided with our wedding anniversary, in late August. As I began the drive back home, I remembered our wedding day. I had woken to crisp sunshine and chilly air on the Columbia Gorge, a scenic place as beautiful as where Jazz was now living. That morning I went for an early run with a friend, and Richard did the same. We laughed and waved, as we were not supposed to see each other before the wedding. At the ceremony, Richard looked nervous and, in fact, his knees were shaking. The ceremony was beautiful and people said afterward they had never felt more love between two people than ours.

The most memorable part of the ceremony was when we went to light candles. Our ceremony took place in a garden in a part of the world known for its considerable winds. We smiled as we lit the candles, not expecting them to burn very long. But the wind stopped unexpectedly, and to everyone's astonishment, the candles stayed lighted for the entire ceremony. Ours was a magical union that burned with an undeniable bright future.

I am sad when I think of my future without Richard in physical form. Someday the girls will marry, and we will miss him profoundly on those days. But even now I feel his light encircling us, embracing and supporting us. Then I had another thought as I continued to drive. This time, I saw an image of the three of us, Jazz, Kenna, and me. We were in a field of grass with mountains around us, yet we were low on the valley floor. We were laughing and holding hands while supporting each other as we went around and around, pulling our arms tight and letting our full body weight fall back as we spun around singly, then rotating in pairs, and finally, all together, like young girls playing on a warm summer day. And we were in joy.

This is the vision I hold, today, for my family as we continue to learn to dance our way to a new family unit.

Three

ACCEPT

… There Is a Divine Order

14.

SOMETIMES LIFE IS UNFAIR

I remembered a time when I once averted danger in a mall parking lot with a *Starsky and Hutch* pose and an invisible gun. I was carrying shopping bags loaded with holiday gifts to my Escalade when I noticed that two large, suspicious-looking men were following me. I picked up my pace. As I put my bags down and bent over to open the car door, I felt a presence come around the back of my car. My instincts kicked in and, still bent, I lunged at him and pointed my finger like a gun. "Stop right there!" I yelled. The man jumped back about seven feet. I bought myself enough time to throw in my packages, get in the driver's seat, lock my door, and drive away. I don't know what would have happened if I had done something different, but I do know that in that moment I had refused to become a victim.

I felt a similar jolt of unexpected strength in the first weeks after Richard died. I went for a walk one morning, the same walk Richard and I had often taken together. It was just after Christmas and I was thinking about how we would be taking the tree down soon, the one Richard lovingly decorated with us with such childlike joy. In a snapshot moment from December 8th (five days before he passed), I turned and looked at Richard trailing a multicolored strand of beads down our Christmas tree. It was a moment that warmed me then, seeing the innocence and wonderment still so visibly present in a grown man. The idea of pulling the beaded garland down saddened my heart as I realized this would be one of hundreds of small ways we would move further away, day by day, from our life together as a complete family.

On this morning my senses were so awakened I could hear the

crackle of every leaf as my foot hit the ground from heel to toe. I was not walking for exercise but rather for a mental break from cabin fever. The branches blew as if all of a sudden there was new life in them, life I had missed before when my mind was busy and I was not present with trees. It began to rain lightly. The cool mist hit my face. I heard water run in the creek with the musical sound of peace that I did not feel inside. I looked up to a blue patch of sky and yearned to fly away from here. That was when I understood the full depth of despair a person could feel. I considered ending this horrible longing, an agony that seemed infinite.

It is not that I was at all *suicidal*, but for the first time in my life, I did have thoughts of dying, too. They would pass in and out of my head as a reminder that I had the option of *opting out*. Of course, I would never abandon my daughters. But, I acknowledged these thoughts and let them pass with the moment. And that is the key – to let them pass.

Holding on to the story of "poor me" would only keep me from moving forward and living *now*. So, I tried to take personal responsibility for my life. After all, personal responsibility was a cornerstone of Richard's teaching as well as one of the most important guiding principles of our lives together. But how do you take personal responsibility for something like this? I thought about this question for days, while sitting alone at night with an unread book in my lap, while getting the girls' breakfast together, and while taking more long walks like this.

Eventually, I decided that personal responsibility in this case meant that I had to start to separate that which was under my control from that which was not, both in the present and in the past. It meant taking responsibility for how to *live on*.

Many new widows I meet talk about their anger as their lives and those of their families tumble into disarray. Some are angry at their dead husbands for abandoning *them*, as though death had been a conscious choice. Initially, I also felt abandoned by Richard. I, too, had walked by his photos and looked at him and cried, "How did you let this happen?"

It was foot-stomping, temper-tantrum kind of angry. It all seemed so unfair.

There were and would always be days where I longed for Richard to be here the way I had always had him. I missed his voice. Sometimes I would listen to one of his books on tape, only a few words, just so I could hear his voice. I would go into his office, where even now his leather jacket still remains wrapped around the arms of his empty office chair, exactly as he left it, where I can sit and fold it around my shoulders for comfort. I would fold a T-shirt from his dirty laundry and keep it in a plastic bag to preserve the scent of him, and I would bury my face and breathe in, taking him in as if I were hugging him tight. When I did those things, I wasn't sure it really helped. Sometimes, I thought it made things worse as I missed him more and came close again to falling into the ditch of feeling sorry for myself.

For a long time, through that winter and well into the summer, I did not stop wishing every day that the outcome was different. I had prayed and dreamed my way out of many things in my life, but this one was irreversible. Finally, that fall, in the beauty and stillness of the season, I let it go. One morning I simply awoke to a different voice. The words were loud and clear: *He didn't leave you, he died.*

Now, what are you going to do about it?

There is nothing fair about death. Sooner or later, we all have to deal with the separation and detachment from form. When I considered our loss from this perspective, I realized it just made things worse because the issue wasn't about fairness. The issue was that he was gone, physically, forever. His form was gone. This life for me was over. I could have controlled that outcome no more than I could have controlled the changing of the seasons, or the traffic lights at the end of our road.

I had to get up. The rest of my life was waiting. This was something I *could* choose. It was all up to me. I could drown in sorrow and anger or accept that fairness robs our lives of the mystery and surprise that make them tick. Wondrous or monstrous, we can find meaning in all things that happen.

I chose the same path Richard would have chosen had our situations been reversed – to gravitate toward joy and seek it in every place I could find it. I also chose to let my feelings come, no matter what they were, to accept them as I accepted the facts as they were, and to be right with them. I knew that resisting what is would only prolong and intensify my grief, including self-pity.

My impression of living a full life means that I must embrace all of it. I cannot pick and choose this but not that. I cannot say I will accept all of the blessings of life and all of life's beauty, without also keeping my heart open to all of life's pain and sorrow. I am committed to living fully alive and awake – this great gift that comes from grieving.

It is what it is, as we used to tell the girls when they were little, after we'd groped for answers to their questions and couldn't come up with a good one. Sometimes we even said that to them when we were tired and impatient. In some ways, the Why? of Richard's death might be one I'd always grope with, too. I began to realize that stepping into my new life would be easier if I stopped tripping over the question, Why did this happen?

It is what it is, I repeated to myself now as I remembered Richard last fall, when his back pain seriously worsened. He would sink into nonresistance, into acceptance; he just went with it. He allowed himself to just be in it. When he did, eventually the pain would subside.

It is what it is, I told myself a year later, when I came, finally, to Acceptance. All pain and emotional suffering comes from wishing things were different than they are. I told myself now what we used to tell Jazz and Kenna when our family was complete and together: Learn to accept life as it is, everything happens. Life is not as you think it should be, expected it would be, or want it to be. It is as it is – for that is the true secret for living a happy contented life.

And now I was ready to step into it.

15.

SEEING IT ALL CLEARLY NOW

Beginning in October, I found my mind in constant review as I accepted my loss. More and more of my freshest memories of Richard were from that period, one year earlier, as he entered the final eight weeks of his life. At first, I worried I would not remember our life together, and then it all seemed to come to me in movie clips like episodes and postscript conversations. I could clearly see things about our life together that I couldn't see when we were living it.

Three years before, during a couple of property moves, Richard's back gave out. It turned out he had a genetic predisposition to back issues, but his tennis-playing years, with their punishing physical workouts, aggravated that condition and set him up for the chronic nerve pain that considerably worsened during the last two years of his life. We sought the help of many surgeons and doctors, but no one could offer any long-term solutions for his collapsed degenerating disks. The girls and I tried to do all we could to support him emotionally, but this was a path Richard struggled on alone hours and hours a day. Periodically, the pain would mysteriously pass, but through the worst of it, he found reprieve and peace from it in his writing.

For the first two years, back pain became a way of life for him as he resolved to power through it, rarely complaining, as though he wanted to make peace with his body using pain as a teacher. Richard saw a Buddhist therapist for support and pain management and thrived under his tutelage. He pursued acupuncture and physical therapy before finally giving in to painkillers and cortisone injections. It really took a lot to knock him down.

Richard's back problems had become a way of life for our family as well, although, looking back on it now, it wasn't until the day of the New Year's mudslide, when a second disk collapsed with a third one disintegrating, that our lives took a sharp turn. There would be no coming back from this, though I couldn't see it then. Over the next several months, Richard hobbled along. There were few good days, only okay and very bad days. Then in October there was a decided change in Richard's attitude and energy. I could feel him pull away. It was ten months after the mudslide, and we had planned a mini-vacation with another couple. Richard's beloved Oakland A's were playing the Seattle Mariners in Seattle; our friends had tickets and we decided to make it a weekend getaway. Two days before we were to leave, Richard woke up in one of the worst bouts of back pain yet. When he looked at me and said he couldn't walk, I knew we had to cancel our trip. He encouraged me to go on without him, but I couldn't leave him; I had never seen him so incapacitated. He looked at me in agony and said in a voice I had never heard before, "I am so sorry, Kris, I just don't think I can do this anymore."

This really terrified me. I felt like he was giving up. Whatever *this* was, it was starting to seem bigger than us. I went to him, bent down on my knees, and laid my head down next to his. I kissed the tips of his fingers and stroked his face with all the love I had ever known: "We'll find something to help you. Hang in there. Please don't ever give up."

I was overcome with dread mixed with panic. My fight mechanism was in full gear. It was Sunday and I pulled out all the stops to get Richard to a doctor first thing Monday morning for a new round of cortisone shots, even though they only took some of the edge off. I could feel him teeter on an edge I would do everything in my power to keep him falling over.

At the time, I had no way of knowing that this was an opening of his spirit to leave, and that Richard was preparing to take it. Eight weeks later, Richard would swiftly depart the body that had betrayed him, discarding it like a well-worn coat that no longer fit.

It amazed me to think that just a couple of years ago we were at the peak of success, the peak of everything. Now Richard was completely disabled. How fast everything had changed, and how fragile the body is. Next to him in bed, I tried to sound positive; maybe I sounded wishful. I told him I was looking forward to a time in our future when his back would recover and we would return to our active lifestyle. Richard just looked at me and smiled and said he, too, looked forward to those days.

The girls and I did all we could and prayed for an answer, for something that would give him relief. It seems our prayers were heard, but the solution did not come in the package we had hoped. On his most difficult days, he withdrew inward, retreated in solitude from the fatigue of pain. There were times I felt lonely. I longed for the easy humor and lighthearted days that seemed to slip away so suddenly.

On a morning hike, alone, I realized our lives were vastly different now and I had been in denial about it. I felt like I was moving through a thick fog; my shoulders were tight as guitar strings. My jaw hurt from clenching my teeth. I would look in the mirror and see fear. I was tired all the time. I distracted myself with lunch dates with girlfriends, retail therapy, driving Jazz and Kenna to their activities, and staying busy. But I was depressed. It was difficult seeing Richard age so quickly and feeling so impotent to help.

Then the pain finally did appear to lift – a new doctor had suggested swimming. Richard hired a swim coach, heated our pool for the winter, and swam every day, which did seem to help – we picked our routines back up again and carried on. Richard rallied and actually felt much better when he left for New York that last time. For two weeks he had been, quite nearly, his old self.

It's so clear to me now: I was complacent, shutting out the reality of what was happening before my eyes. I wasn't feeling life deeply or completely as I buried myself in habit and distractions. I allowed myself to go numb instead of giving myself the freedom to experience my feelings as I watched Richard suffer and witnessed the changes in our life as a couple. I only fully understood the depth of my slumber when I felt the contrast of a sudden, deep awakening within days of Richard's transition, as grief shot through me like a lightning bolt.

With my memories now taking on an unexpected poignancy as these fall days tracked against Richard's final eight weeks, I looked at our life in a way I never had before. It was like being hit in the face with water, cold and violent from a fully pressurized fire hose.

And I could not turn away.

Richard was one of those people who walked the talk, every day. He never saw himself as a best-selling author, a visionary, or a master teacher – only an ordinary guy who knew some common-sense things about being a kind, gentle, loving, and present person. He was a willing instrument driven to do his part to create well-being on the planet, and believed that leading individuals to inner peace is one step on the way to world peace – one person at a time. His therapy and writing were rooted in connecting to the divine and then, simply, expressing it in his own words which would help millions of people around the globe live better.

One of the great burdens Richard carried was living up to his book titles. He felt enormous pressure always to be authentic. But how does a man who gives advice to the world, who has been happy for the most part his whole life, struggle himself? He always took personal responsibility for his own happiness or unhappiness, and the truth is, no person is happy all the time, but the pressure always to be that which he wrote about never escaped his radar.

We built our careers (mine originally in graphic design) step by step, sharing an intense work ethic and sense of purpose. We spent our early married life, like all couples, mapping out the strategy to achieve our dreams of a fulfilling family, spiritual, material, and professional life. It took a little longer than we expected, but after ten years our life seemed almost charmed. By then I was with the girls full-time, and Richard had produced ten books. He was interviewed on *Oprah* four times and appeared on nearly every national television news show around the country. There were magazine covers and newspaper profiles; *People* identified him as a breakout talent in 1998. Richard's little book, *Don't Sweat the Small Stuff*, had done what no book ever had: become the number one best-selling book in America for two years in a row. We were in spiritual alignment and our hearts were pure. We used to laugh and tell each other to enjoy the ride now because life gives you just enough joy to get you through to the next round, where the lessons of growth could challenge us any number of ways. How prescient that was.

With two little daughters in elementary school, life was like a science project, and if you have children you know what I'm talking about. They grew, but Richard's career grew even faster. He was in high gear and high demand. We rode the wave of success, though we did our best to keep our family life stable and grounded. Richard had to write his work and be "Richard Carlson," and my job was to be in service to my family – to run the household and to make sure Richard had a safe place to land. For a long time, our lives flourished, and as our girls got older, our marriage remained solid and connected; we were truly happy. We lived our lives with a shared intimacy; we walked side by side, but there were times we carried each other, too.

After a few years, I walked into our living room and discovered Richard sitting with his head in hands, bent over, frustrated, and in tears. Booked solid, traveling sometimes four days a week several times a month, and under deadline to write two more installments in his *Don't Sweat* series, he was overwhelmed with obligations and had no time to actually write. He paced frantically. Then he stopped and looked at me searchingly. "What happened to my life? Where do I fit into this chaos? A reader wrote to me and asked where I go to get my insights, like am I in the mountains writing somewhere or something? My God, I can't even go to the bathroom without my cell phone ringing. I write my books on the foldout table of an airplane seat. I am always missing you and the girls. What do I do? I feel like I'm going completely insane while I am supposed to inspire others to calm down!"

We spent the next several hours talking, unpacking his worries and agonies, as we looked to understand how we had gotten here. I began to witness a subtle shift in him that was a manifestation of this distress. I knew better than anyone that he wrote from his heart and his passion, and he knew that meeting the public and promoting his books were part of the business of book writing. But it was a treadmill on which he did not thrive. All that promoting did not exactly nourish his soul, and in fact he loathed selling. He didn't do it for the fame and attention. He wrote because early in life he was called to his mission to teach what he knew about being a happy person. He became a household name, but straddled the world between living *in* his own wisdom and sharing it through his work. That balance was gone in the wake of success.

Richard had let his professional life take its own course and he didn't have a sense of control anymore; he was no longer navigating from inner peace and presence. I tried to help bring him back to his own life and restore some equilibrium. "What parts of this do you feel you can do or need to do, and what parts can you say no to?" I asked. We talked about our priorities as a family, and how he could begin to set limits and boundaries in his career; he had earned that luxury.

Over the next few years, he pulled his reins in, and traveled less. He began to say, "No, thank you," and "I am on writing hiatus." He wrote a book a year and promoted one a year and dialed back his speaking engagements. He continued to help new authors in their careers by writing forewords to their books, offering endorsements, and by coaching people at a crossroads in their lives without a fee, all as a way to give back some of the good fortune he was so grateful for.

The pathway of grief breaks through a wall around the heart. It opens us to see life from a different perspective. The mist of denial and the fog that shrouded the last two years finally rolled out. The air turned luminous with the clarity of my awakened state; and the truth of our lives as they really were held me spellbound.

Richard yearned for the simple life that he encouraged other people to have, but it somehow seemed to escape him. In some ways our personalities were opposite, and I was temperamentally far better geared to live the public life that he was thrust into. He didn't care much about the material part of life, and I did. I was so grounded in my responsibilities that I didn't see that we could choose to live out of the box and do life differently. I think if it were up to Richard we would have lived more adventurously; we would have taken the kids out of school and traveled instead of rooting ourselves so deeply in a community.

Life called Richard out too far, and he had a difficult time accepting all the chaos. Increasingly, he yearned to live on the coast, away from the Bay Area. I told him that in the next phase of our life we would go where he wanted to live. He would direct the next segment, after the children were grown. In the last year of his life, he could feel his writing career winding down and spoke of deepening his work with a foundation involving literacy and children. Richard spent ninety percent of every day in service to others. Whether it was his family, friends and colleagues, or his readers, he spent very little time in consideration of himself.

Our life seemed to be inching positively forward again. Richard was feeling better and exercising in the pool, and I remember him sitting in the driveway thumbing through his mail one afternoon as I drove up. He gave me a wide smile, and I thought how glad he must be to be living his life again. Life was back on track until two weeks before he died, when there was a treacherous moment.

Richard was at our house at Sea Ranch, where he often went to write. He was extremely focused and had the intensity of very deep presence; he could go there and write the better part of a book in fourteen days. This was also his very special place; at Sea Ranch he could relax and be the way he wanted to be, unencumbered by expectations and the pulls of public life. He loved the wide-open space of the ocean.

At Sea Ranch there is a secret beach with a precipitous coastline and deep rocky crevices. Richard was climbing over the rocks and spotted a baby octopus wedged in between two rocks. As he reached up to un-wedge it, the rock fell back on him, he lost his balance, and fell down into the water. It was so scary – he went in and was fully immersed. Looking back, I believe he fought for his life that day. He was in shock as he peeled his clothes off and immediately went to sleep. He looked pale and he couldn't talk about it.

The next two weeks felt heavy for me. I remember feeling a depressed foreboding laced with anxiety and fear. Instead of facing it, I swatted it away. He had been lucky he hadn't injured his back further; he was lucky to be alive. Everything was fine.

I see now that God had a new plan for Richard and was calling him. Throughout his life, Richard's vibration was high. He always had a hard time sleeping; the energy of that man was so great and the light in him so evident. It's almost as though he did know at some level he wasn't going to live a long life. He did all the things he dreamed about, with his children, with his work; the letter he wrote me that became *An Hour to Live, an Hour to Love* told me everything I needed to know about his feelings for me and about the life we had shared. But during those last eight weeks of his life, these tendencies all accelerated. He visited every-one who was important to him. He taped a schedule inside a kitchen cabinet listing the medications our family dog, Ty, was taking along with the dosages, almost as a reminder for us, as if he knew he was not going to be here to do it as he always did.

Richard lived every day as though he could die at any time, doing all the things he taught others to do. "Picture yourself at your own memorial service," he once wrote. He believed that if you keep the idea of your mortality close, it helps you to live a better, more present, and more complete life. He left us notes in places we would find them. The day before he died, he left a note on the driver's seat of my car: "Kris, you are everything to me. I love you so much. Thank you for being my partner."

Now I see that Richard was resisting leaving his family. I see that in the mudslide and in our canceled Seattle holiday. I see that in his close call at Sea Ranch. Richard didn't want to die, but his personal foundation was somehow slipping and the house for his spirit weakening, one lumbar disk at a time.

Only now, looking back, can I see the layers and symbolism, the depth and density of life, how they track and intermingle. Everything is a continuation and not just about the single event that happens – it's how they get woven together. I understand that I lost myself in that last year. After the mudslide I felt exhaustion and fear and helplessness as I watched Richard resist, and I couldn't do anything to stop it. A part of me saw what was unfolding, but I didn't want to believe it. I lost him, and I woke up.

Even in death Richard taught what he taught in life; he was about living as if you could walk out the door and not return. He did not take anything for granted.

16.

THE ROLE OF REGRET

As we begin the grief process, there is a part of us that wants to get control and power back, and we think we can do that through our regrets. For months I looked at Richard's pictures, at our children, at our life together and I couldn't believe that a man filled with so much life had actually died. During those last few months, when I saw that something about his energy and awareness was different, when I felt him disconnecting, I was a little perplexed, and even a bit angry. Now I understand all too well that I was responding to a really big spiritual shift that was taking place, that I had no control over.

But when something happens out of your control, you go through a renegotiation. A friend reminded me that when we love, we love without boundaries. Her dog suffered from his dysplasia and had to be put down. As she spoke about her dog, who had been her dearest companion during the happiest and most difficult years of her life, she said, "I wish I had taken better care of him. I should have given him more attention." It reminded me of my own thinking and how I was trying to renegotiate what happened with Richard. But you have to make peace with what you can't take back and would change if you could. Regret is a normal part of grief and we must remember there is no peaceful resolution to it outside acceptance and self-understanding. It is the ego's talon holding us in a position of resistance. We cannot change our past. We can only move forward and learn from it.

Most of us live unconsciously and don't realize how precious every moment is until it's gone. As much as I knew about how I should be living, I didn't always follow what I knew. Living with awareness and gratitude is a choice that we have to make every second of every day. It is far easier to rest and slumber. Richard was very careful always to make sure we knew how much he loved us. Although I often verbalized my feelings of gratitude for his hard work and my love for him, I did not leave him a note or have time to speak with him that fateful morning, so in vulnerable moments I ask myself: Did he die knowing how much I loved him? Deep down, I knew he did, but the last days you spend with someone can dangle in the air like the smell of smoke after a fire. We were so busy and rushed with a book tour, end-of-semester school projects, launching a new website, and preparation for the holidays.

Many questions gnawed at me and came at me, like toy soldiers with bayonets coming over a hill in wave after wave of attack. I'd answer one question and then a new assault would start. Could I have done more for Richard? Could I have shown him more support? Did I love him well enough? How could I have stood by and not seen there was something wrong? What kind of wife was I anyway?

Sometimes my mind floated back across time. It was fall of last year again, Jazz's senior year. Before we knew it, it was Thanksgiving. There was so much going on. Did we stop to think, really think, about how much we had to be grateful for? I couldn't remember. We were grateful Richard was back on his feet, able to step into his life again, and then he died. It took time, but eventually I understood there was not much about that I could have negotiated. I couldn't mend the results of this. Sometimes we can go back to people and say, "I'm sorry, can I try it again? Can I do something to make you feel better now?" All I could tell myself was the truth: As Richard's wife, I was worried; I was concerned. No matter what I did right, or if there was anything I might have done differently in the landscape of our many years together and in the tall tree country of those final weeks, I had to believe with certainty Richard died knowing he was completely loved, and I would have to leave it there.

Regret teaches us how to look at ourselves. We search our faces and see our blemishes, but we also see the reminders of our youthful, most hopeful selves. And perhaps we see a hard-won wisdom. Surely, there are pieces of my life with Richard I would do differently now that I am in an awakened state. I could have encouraged him to get out of that two-book contract. I might have followed him to another corner of the world, where we could have lived more simply and raised our daughters outside the pressure cooker that is so ingrained in suburban life. I might have.

I realize the futility of such circular thinking. Those haunting questions lead me to the same place: a mountain I cannot move. And so, I jump each thought like a hurdle to acceptance. When the toy soldiers in my mind come over the rise with their swords drawn, I tell myself this: "Two people could not have done a better job loving each other every day than we." We were everything love should be. Had we done life differently, Richard might have lived longer. But that is not the life Richard chose for himself. He chose to live in the trenches, where he could feel the grittiness of life, and teach *because* he lived as a hungry student in its very fold. If we found ourselves on a treadmill we at least had the wisdom to know we were on a treadmill. Yet part of being a teacher is living a real life, and we were in the thick of living family life. On those days of self-torture, when I find it hard to forgive myself for what I might have done or did not do, that is what I remind myself. Richard loved his work; teaching meant everything to him. I believe he fulfilled his purpose here. Without a real life, there would have been nothing to teach. He lived, and died, the way he wanted.

Moving past regret is to accept the nonnegotiable, but not to disavow it.

One of my biggest regrets that I struggle with now is that I cannot be in this world living life with Richard from this awakened state. The shock of his death pulled all the blankets off and knocked me out of my slumber into a completely alert, altered state. I can do nothing about that now. I can only shift how I understand and see life. Now I can bring back the passionate girl that Richard fell in love with into the fullness that life has given me as a woman.

Richard often said that circumstances of life don't make you, they reveal you. It is the sum of our experiences, good and bad, that *brings* us to who we are. My journey through grief has shown me that I am connected to the earth and to anyone who is open to connection. I am grounded. I am strong. I have the courage of a warrior and the wisdom of a shaman. I wouldn't have known I was like this if I hadn't lost Richard.

We were so close to having the time to rediscover our connection, as couples do when their kids are grown and they reach midlife. It pains me that he set our lives up so beautifully and now he can't enjoy it. The guilt I feel and my deepest regret is that he lived for everyone and especially for me; he gave me so much. I have the rest of my life ahead of me, and I am going to live it without him. And yet, I thank God that Regret has shown me how much life I have left inside me, and how much I want to share this awakened state with everyone I love in the here and now.

17.

HOLDING THE PERFECT LIFE

From the time we moved into our new home three years before Richard died, he wanted me to have his closet. The couple who built our house had beautiful taste but were minimalists. I had to dramatically downsize my closet, which proved to be a good thing for several of my girlfriends. Divided by a hallway, my closet was on the left, Richard's was on the right. Richard said, "Kris, take mine, too, and I will build one in the garage."

The garage? I thought as I rolled my eyes. Did he really say that? "No, honey." I refused. "You must have your own closet. I will not take your space."

Perhaps this is why it took me so long to begin to remove Richard's clothes. At first, it was hard for me to see his things. His clothing was a reminder that he had just been here. His personal records were also there. So was the box with his ashes and the goofy "Life Is Good" T-shirts Richard adored wearing. The signs of his life were painful; as time went on his scent grew more intense, or maybe my awareness was so much stronger. But I wouldn't move anything; I didn't touch anything; everything was exactly as he left it.

After a few months, with my own things crushed together as always in my closet – Richard always shuddered a bit at the mess whenever he walked by – I started to move a few things of my own in, without moving him out. It had been so long since I was in there that I looked at everything, item by item. I picked up his jeans and as I remembered his body, I marveled at his size. Most of his favorite button-down shirts bore a permanent stain in the center because Richard always ate on the run in his car and typically spilled his food or drink down the front. This makes me smile because in these ways Richard remained very innocent. Each shirt showed signs of a good life.

Everyone told me "you'll know" when the time is right to let go. That fall I began to take some small steps in removing Richard's things. I knew I wasn't ready to let everything go. It struck me hard right after his death how awful it was to remove his name from the bills and the trail of paper that followed us, paper that Richard spent so much time having to maintain and shuffle around. He would disappear; to the gas and electric companies it would be as though he had never existed.

Letting go would have to come in layers.

It struck me, as I examined my life now versus the old one I fell out of nearly a year ago, that our closets are containers for the perfect, ordered life we thought we had and the new, messy one my family inhabited now. It surprised me how grief shattered that illusion of our perfect family. It surprised me how much easier that was to let go.

There had been a time in life, before Richard's final turn, when I would look at my perfect life and wonder, "What's the matter with you?" Why couldn't I feel happy, or at least why was I so lethargic? Where had my passion gone? My sense of purpose? While the changes in Richard's deteriorating health brought transition to our lives, my feelings were far more fundamental, far more systematic than that.

Pinched and knotted from holding life, my shoulders were often shored up like vises. Somewhere I had gotten lost in my life as Richard's wife and Jazz and Kenna's mom. For a long time, that had been enough. Then it became *everything*. I had willingly closed my graphic design business and traded that in for parks, play dates, and pb&j sandwiches when the girls were little. But they were growing now. Richard was deeply engaged in his work. When I was quiet, a voice in my head kept asking me a nagging question: "Where do I fit into my own life?"

Still, our days and nights were a fast-running stream. The girls had their school and their sports. They had hours and hours of homework.

Richard had his traveling and his books. I was at the center of it all, making sure everyone had what they needed to keep it all working like a well-tuned clock. Our schedule as a family was exhaustion itself. When I looked back at the wall calendar, I was shocked by my tight, cramped handwriting as each day was stacked with activity; each little box marking the day was filled to the point of overflow. It was a chop-chop schedule where every minute counted and there was no longer time for family dinners or special events like birthdays. With two kids in year-round sports, we were on the run after school every day from 3:00 to 7:00 P.M., and then it was a race to open the books and turn out the lights. All to begin the insane hamster wheel again the following day. Weekends were taken up with soccer tournaments and cheerleading competitions and, always, more homework.

Richard and I could see the futility of putting our daughters through what seemed like insurmountable pressure to perform to standards of perfection that more often than not produced troubled, exhausted, and unhappy kids, yet we could not figure a way out. We were aware how difficult it was to get into good colleges, and how parents feed on that fear and pressure. It was contagious. You can't stop or slow down, because you might find your child bumped off track. And, of course, it would somehow be *your* fault.

I look back at the frenzy of those years, and I can see that I was feeling my responsibility to run the household and keep things steady at such a deep level that I became lost in it. My enthusiasm and passion dwindled in the weight of schedules and "to-do" lists. I had a hard time combining my spiritual, passionate side with the practical side. It's hard to find your passion when you are changing diapers and driving children and raising teenagers. You live in spirit day to day, but I couldn't always see and feel that. I wasn't feeling *my* life. As women and gatherers, we get caught up in making the perfect life for our family.

Not judging myself too harshly, by most standards I looked and acted happy and I, too, thought I was. I threw myself into volunteer work; I served on committees. I exercised and shopped and met with girlfriends. And then at three o'clock I got into the car, and the crazy rat-race pace that was stealing our time together as a family would begin again. All of this, I thought, gave me a sense of freedom, but even then, I often felt something was missing. I would say to myself, *"Something is wrong, I'm not living right."* Now I can see how much of my life energy was ultimately spent in distraction from a feeling of emptiness. While I was steadfast in my commitment to marriage and family, something inside me wasn't feeling life completely.

Richard's death swiftly pulled me out of the closet of my illusions. All of my deepest fears became reality that day. And once your fear becomes reality, there's no point in fearing it anymore. When Richard died, my core sense of self – *Kris as Richard's wife* – died with him. It was wrought with sorrow, but in an unexpected way, Richard's death was a beautiful gift. His death opened me to rediscover myself in the passionate place of the world. A deeper awakening forced open by grief brought me back into fertile growth.

By that fall, a part of me had died, too – this self who had become so tightly wound I changed dramatically. I began to live in creativity rather than complacency. I disengaged from the pettiness I saw around me. I slowed down and tuned in. I became aware of my feelings, so much so that I became aware of all the ways I wasn't aware before. I felt the blessings of everything that was right instead of noticing all the things that were wrong. I stopped worrying so much or trying to hold on too tightly. Most importantly, I stopped identifying with my life in the ways I used to.

The awakening – how else to explain it? – became clear to me that spring as I sat beside dear friends at the eighth-grade graduation of their son, my godson. I saw things differently this May of 2007. I took a good look around. To me, every family appeared perfectly intact as I noticed all the mothers and fathers in attendance with their proud, eager expressions. I remembered how the year before Richard and I had sat together at our Kenna's eighth-grade promotion. Then, out of nowhere, a thought occurred to me as I considered the ramped-up expectations that lay ahead of them: Ninth grade "really" mattered, or so we all believed. From here on, it would all be about ensuring a future that couldn't be controlled. I thought about the shrinking family time, and the late nights of homework, the exhaustion that would spread across the entire family, like a virus, by trying to do it all much too well. And then I thought with relief, *I am no longer holding the perfect life* or living in any kind of illusion that I can control life. We are off the treadmill now, I realized. Richard's death gifted us with a clear opening off the hamster wheel and into a different way of life.

As the new school term began that fall, I felt myself relax in ways I hadn't in months. I was *letting go*. I no longer had the perfect life to hold; mine was already in pieces. My goals and perspective changed as I embraced life as it is outside the container of cultural expectations with their impossible goals and wrongheaded priorities. Letting go let us come back to ourselves.

As I released the illusion of the perfect family, I felt the rhythm of life change from fast to slow, and like a river the current changed inside me with my emotions. I learned to check in with myself and notice how I was feeling, and to listen to my body and my spirit. I noticed there was more space between my thoughts, as I was not busy-minded most of the time. I found that when I would deal with things as they arose – and there was much to take care of – I was never overtaxed by any one thing. Even the business stuff that I thought would completely overwhelm me worked out just fine as long as I did what was right in front of me.

Nature has never looked more brilliant as my sorrow opened me to seeing it with new eyes widened with awe. As my identity shattered, my presence increased and so did my inner light. I was no longer secure in the protective womb of my husband's shadow, a place where I found it easy to hide. As I let go of the roles, habits, and stories that had created a Kris Carlson I no longer recognized, passion returned. And so did a more contented, determined, and purposeful me.

There are many ways my loss has simplified my way of life. By living in the moment, I am not consumed with pleasing others or whether or not the details of life are going to work out perfectly. I am far more accepting of what *is*, even when things don't appear to be going smoothly. And, my closet is still a mess! I also don't worry about taking care of other people's emotional needs like I used to. If a relationship is not nourishing, I don't choose to participate in anything that will potentially drain me.

I have learned that fear is a way of holding on rather than letting go. The most pain we can encounter in life is detaching from the people we love. We can detach from our money, our homes, even our dreams. But when death comes so cruelly, the natural order is upset. There is nothing harder. We don't move on from our loved ones, but we do move forward.

Letting go comes in layers. That fall I had a desire to organize our things and I started with one closet at a time. I arranged to donate some of Richard's clothing. But I decided to send his favorite shirts to a quilt artist I know. She will design three lap-size quilts with these shirts and perhaps embroider them with his book titles.

I don't sweat the small stuff. I have learned to let go of the little things. I have discovered time flies fast, and life changes in a heartbeat.

18.

WOMAN TO WOMAN

It was Friday night, mid-July, and a girlfriend called to see if I wanted to get a salad and listen to some live music. I loathed sitting home on the weekends, and jumped at the chance to get out. It was a nice evening, and our conversation took an intimate turn to sex. She asked me what it was like to go so long without it. I confided it was making me crazy because I felt tremendous energy swirling in my body, and I felt like I wanted sex all the time. The night that I had spent with my special friend, the one with benefits, was quick and had only temporarily appeased my ascending libido. I wasn't sure if that was going to happen again or anytime soon. My girlfriend said that since she turned forty, she felt that her sex drive was also on the rise, and that her husband could barely keep up with her. I felt such deep envy because I could no longer share intimate moments with my husband. I asked her jokingly if she would lend me hers for a few minutes. She laughed and said, "Sorry, Kris, but I don't share. I have an idea though; let's go."

We pulled up to a store in a strip mall called Sweet Vibrations, where I noticed people got out of their cars, kept their heads down, and didn't make eye contact. As we stepped inside and looked around, I had an uneasy feeling laced with a bit of excitement, almost like I was engaging in something *bad*. Then I began getting the giggles. Richard and I had never experimented with "sex toys." I could never think of any reason we needed them. But several of my married friends were beginning to dive into alternative sources of pleasure to spice things up in the bedroom.

I was now a single woman, but my libido wasn't interested in my marital status. That night, my friend bought me my first vibrator as a belated birthday gift. Since her husband was out of town, we both agreed to try out our new toys and call each other the next morning. I laugh to myself even now that it took me all of a minute and a half to feel satisfied.

The truth is, throughout my marriage, I had grown unaccustomed to touching my own body and it felt awkward to me. I stood in front of the mirror before my nightly bath, stared down the length of my body, and tried to see it the way a stranger would. I held my shoulders back and square as they looked hunched and rounded, and I noticed I looked a little, well, older. I knew I was still a very attractive woman, but the woman staring back at me was just not the trim, firm young girl she'd once been. I knew Richard loved every inch of me, just as I was. But as a newly single woman, my insecurities and loneliness flared; I heard my ego like a goblin in the back of my head as it taunted, "What man will find you attractive? You are going to be *alone!*"

It was as much of a surprise to me that I had all of these feelings as it was that my body was stirring like a pot of boiling water. When Richard was alive, I had grown to accept my body and allowed myself the space to age naturally and healthily. Now I felt stripped of my sense of security as I pondered the idea that there would be a time, someday, when another man whom I could love would enter my life. I wondered what that would be like and how I would appear to him.

I began to think this could be a long while, so I'd better get comfortable with my body on my own. There are the realities of being a woman and a sexual being. I had gone from my childhood home to a "first love" to meeting Richard at Pepperdine. There hadn't been a lot of men. What I'd learned about my body I learned through lovemaking with Richard. I was so young when we fell in love.

But losing Richard opened me to something new. Here was one more way I learned to take care of myself. I found that taking care of my own body was self-empowering, and it also kept me from engaging in risky sexual encounters that other single women I knew were prone to. I was surprised to find an opportunity beyond the secure life of marriage and sexual commitment to one man for twenty-five years. The opportunity has been to learn how to make love to myself.

19.

SIZE FIFTEEN SHOES

In the eleventh month of my grief, I found myself once more boarding a plane. This would be my third overseas flight this year. Unlike our trips to India and Sweden, the girls were not with me. This time, I was going alone.

I had heard about a well-regarded, professionally run spiritual workshop being given in Verona, Italy, called The Path of Love. With the publication of *An Hour to Live, An Hour to Love* nearing, the national publicity being planned already included an appearance on *Oprah* as well as other media. I was excited and deeply honored, but I was terribly apprehensive, too; I knew it would be a challenge to sit on national television and be vulnerable and exposed. I hoped that The Path of Love would advance my healing so I would be able to speak personally and publicly about my life with Richard. My friend Lisa was going to attend the workshop with me.

On the morning of our flight, as the driver pulled out of the driveway, he turned to us and joked, "You ladies have your passports?" We laughed and said of course we did. However, when we arrived at the terminal and went to check in for the overnight flight, Lisa's passport was missing. She nervously leafed through her travel documents, her carry-on bag, her suitcase – everything, and ... *nothing*. "I can't believe this!" she said as she looked through her things a second time. "I'm sure I have it. I know I'll find it!"

I took her luggage as she tried to call home, sat down, and waited. I was dead calm. I knew after fifteen minutes she was not going to find that passport. She walked over to me and slumped down in a cold sweat and cried, "Kris, I'm so sorry this happened and it is going to ruin our trip."

I looked at her and put my arms around her and told her, "No, honey. It's going to ruin *your* trip! I'm still going."

Shocked, she smiled and said, "You are going *alone?*" Though surprised, she was clearly happy about my decision – a decision that required some courage given the circumstances. For me to go on this trip without Lisa felt like a child losing her security blanket, as Lisa very much represents partnership and safety to me.

My resolve to go alone did not come from thinking it through. Rather, it came from a deep serenity within. *Surrender, trust and accept.* In this year of firsts, I was learning to be a single parent to my daughters. There had been a romance, a book, new friends, and now this travel – each a risk. Grief had already opened me to a greater capacity for love, compassion, and expression. Somehow, I knew now that I was meant to navigate this particular piece of my journey myself. The workshop would break me down one more time and build me up again. I would know no one there. I would discover, as nothing else had shown me in quite the same way in this long year, just how far I'd come.

"Well," I laughed as I kissed Lisa good-bye, "the workshop has already started."

On the way over, my spontaneous wall of confidence collapsed as I began to think about the enormity of what was just ahead between the workshop and the book tour. This time, fear nearly cracked me. I looked out the window at the night sky. The horizon had already disappeared and with it, I slipped back into memory. There was another time when I had been deeply afraid, too, and had found my way. I looked into the inky pool of darkness and pondered my thoughts, lost in reverie. Would that help me this time?

It started with what Richard thought would be great news to me. We had just completed our national tour for a book we coauthored,

Don't Sweat the Small Stuff in Love, and our publisher was extremely pleased with the results. Richard asked me how I felt now that it was over and I replied, "I'm relieved to be done. I want to get back to normal life with the girls."

Richard said, "Well, maybe not so fast. The publisher was really impressed with you. They want you to write a book in the series for women."

My eyes widened and my stomach somersaulted. All I could say was "Really?" and then what I said surprised even me, "What if I don't want to?" He was seated across the kitchen table from me, sitting the way he did when he was relaxed, one leg crossed over his ankle, his thumb massaging his cleft chin. He leaned forward and looked at me with a gentle yet unwavering gaze. There was no judgment in his voice as he replied, "That surprises me. Why wouldn't you want to write *Don't Sweat the Small Stuff for Women?*"

I had so much fear I didn't know where to begin. Mostly it came down to my worry that I'd be seen as a wife riding my husband's coattails. What made me qualified to give anyone advice on how to live their life? I had no "Doctor" next to my name. But then Richard helped me reframe that. "Kris, our books are only meant to offer examples through our life and to show options to people on how to choose to be kinder, take better care of themselves and others, to communicate more clearly and live from their hearts. These are all things you do every day. There isn't a woman in the world who would write a book for women in this series better than you, because you live it. You are it." He took my hand and raised it to his lips. "But, if you really don't want to, I'll find someone else. Just sit on it for a day or so and see how you feel. I really hope you decide to write it, though."

Oh man, was I scared. I used to look at Richard and wonder how the shy college boy I'd met all those years ago now spoke with such confidence in front of thousands of people. I had loved working together on this last book. I'd even enjoyed promoting it. It was beautiful the way we danced through an interview always in touch with each other. Just by a look we signaled - *this question is yours* - and every interview showed our love for each other. Our cohesive relationship was evident and our harmony obvious. But that would be different if I did this book. The content would be mine. I'd be exposing a great deal. I wasn't the experienced writer Richard was, nor the promoter. His were impossibly big shoes to fill.

And yet, I knew I had to do it. I would have felt like I had failed in some way if I didn't meet this challenge. And so, I started by writing every day for one hour. I would sit at my computer and I wouldn't know what was going to come. My kids would leave for school; Richard would go to his office. I picked up the house and did the breakfast dishes, threw in a load of laundry, and then sat down to meditate. "Dear God," I would quietly ask, "play me like a fiddle. Show me what to write today." And then I would sit down at the computer and go. I finished the book in about six months. My editor was thrilled; Richard was, too. And so was I. I'd found a voice and a gift that otherwise would have remained hidden in my fears.

That was the easy part.

When spring 2001 came, *Don't Sweat the Small Stuff for Women* had a national lay-out date and a one-hundred-thousand-copy first printing. That gave me one hundred thousand reasons to be nervous. A new national tour was planned. Every day I was getting closer to stepping into my husband's shoes, at his level, in his arena. Every day I was a little more scared.

The day before I was scheduled to do a satellite tour of morning news shows, I flew to Los Angeles to meet with media coaches for the day, a not uncommon support that publishers arrange for new authors. The satellite tour would allow me to do fifty interviews of three to five minutes each from one studio and they were to begin very, very early the next morning to accommodate all of the East Coast markets first, before making our way through the other time zones.

Media coaching had sounded like a good idea to get my strategies in line before the interviews, and to learn how to deflect criticism or hard-to-answer questions from an imaginary hostile host. But as I sat with the coaches, and they talked back and forth to each other, parsing my every response, I felt dread building somewhere in my core. I hate role-playing. I disliked the idea of practiced response – and as I sat there for hours trying to please these coaches, I felt overwhelmed and full of dread. This was going to be a disaster.

I left the five-hour session with a lot of notes and preparation and their expectation that I was going to show up the next morning as someone other than who I am - some made-up version of me. I went to bed at 7:30 that night after studying all the strategies they gave me, and I awoke to my alarm at 1:00 A.M. I rang the room service button to order coffee. When the person on the other end answered, "Hello, this is room service, what can I get you this morning?" I opened my mouth to speak, but not even one small sound came out. I swallowed and tried again. There was nothing but croaking air. I coughed and hoped that might clear my throat, but I couldn't make a peep. I had no voice. I had never had laryngitis before in my life.

True panic swept over me as I ran downstairs to have someone call the publicist in charge. I wrote a note for the desk clerk to read into the phone because not even my whisper was audible. They canceled all the interviews and I was on a plane home by 8:00 A.M. Richard tried to comfort me and said, "Things happen, Kris, don't worry." I felt like a failure and yet, I was relieved beyond words. I felt somehow spared - but not for long. The whole thing was rescheduled for one week later. I thought to myself, *You have some work to do, girl.*

I began an internal workshop during my forced days of silence and started by asking what part of this I was most afraid of. I was deeply afraid I wasn't good enough and wasn't qualified by any official standard beyond being Richard Carlson's wife and life partner. Most of all, I was deeply afraid of not being myself. The media coaching only enforced my fears. I ripped all my notes to ribbons and was determined to start over.

I spent several days not thinking about what I would say but focusing instead on quieting my mind and assuaging my fears by shedding light on the areas that I was most afraid of. One week later, my voice returned and I flew back to Los Angeles. I sat down in front of the camera ready to answer any question now from my heart. I focused on something Richard had told me as I listened that week, something he had learned years before as he prepared to promote his early books. "It's not what you say. It's how it feels inside when you say it," he told me. "It gives an audience permission to feel that feeling in you. The feeling you give them, rather than the words themselves, is what they remember." So, I set aside the advice of the media coaches who were asking me to be someone else. I showed up as me. The interviews were fantastic. And I learned that being real is the most comfortable place you can be … even in front of national TV.

***

I arrived in Verona refreshed by the reminder of what past experience had already taught me and ready to receive all the healing the workshop could inspire. I spent my days throughout that week in deep exercise and contemplation. In my free time, I would sit in the garden or stare out the picture windows in the old remodeled villa. There is nothing like the Italian countryside under a glistening late autumn sun. Here was a living portrait of perfection: posted grapevines and tolling church bells that offered me peace and comfort inside. But the great gift of the workshop for me was the process of *going* to Verona itself. It amazed me that I had intuited my own healing through expression - through music, meditation, movement, and so much more. I had done it in ways that were in alignment with and enriched by the workshop's distinctive and highly creative process.

My own path of healing presented a far more extensive and expansive curriculum than I could have devised, but what I found at the Path of Love validated that I had chosen the right path for me. By living in a very deep process, as I had been since that terrible first shattered day, I had experienced a kind of transformative healing as I shook out my grief and sat in stillness with it.

Day after day I had shown up as myself.

My week in Verona reminded me what I had already learned. We need only to release our feelings as they are, to live in full expression. And, I discovered, it was a beautiful thing that I had done this important piece alone. Having my girlfriend there would have inhibited my freedom of expression. The fact that I ended up going alone allowed me to embrace my biggest fear. I was so afraid of being alone, and here I was uninterrupted by expectations or any kind of boundaries.

Exactly one week after I returned from Italy, I flew to Chicago to tape *Oprah*, the kickoff for the national publicity for *An Hour to Live, An Hour to Love* but, more important, the national tribute to my beloved. It now seemed very clear to me that neither Richard, nor God, wanted me to show up as someone else. When Oprah played a tape of Richard to introduce our segment, I had to grab my heart. I hadn't seen him outside a photograph in eleven months and here he was on a large screen, alive and vital. I did what came to me as naturally as breath. There is no script for feelings; authenticity needs no practice. I cried. Oprah asked me as she gently touched my hand for support, "Are you able to continue?" Briefly, I allowed my grief to rock me as I had been so afraid to do in front of the studio audience and before the millions of viewers who would be watching when the show aired next month. I took a very deep breath, gathered myself, and nodded. And I moved forward, just as that year of "firsts" had shown me how to do.

For months Richard's size fifteen shoes seemed too big for me to fit into. He had accomplished so much during his short lifetime, and shoes are symbolic of holding the person. Now I saw it differently. I had always deferred my dreams to him and therefore I thought our life was magical and amazing because *he* was. I always thought he was the dreamer and the creator and that *I* was along for the ride. Now I see that fifty percent of the beautiful life Richard and I created was *me*. I can see this now because I have been successful at carrying on. I am Richard and he is me. Part of what he created was because I created it with him.

I never gave myself the kind of credit he gave me. He was always trying to push me forward to stand by his side, not three steps behind where I could hide in his shadow.

Today, I am learning that with each step I take, I am stepping more into me. I see that my shoes need be no bigger than my own size seven. They need only to carry my own weight and to leave my own impressions.

20.

DIVINE ORDER

There is a time when grief, like a comet with a long fiery tail, burns itself out.

The last hurdle for me came in December as we prepared to mark the second anniversary of Richard's passing. Through the past years, I had no deep desire to imagine his last moments. I did not want to become lost in the details of that story. I never wanted to be distracted that way, but now something told me that to move forward, it was time to look backward; that I was ready, that I was strong, and that my life and Richard's were united still in life's Divine Order.

Wouldn't it be nice if we could turn the clock back? How many times we tell ourselves this. In grief it is almost an incantation, and there were many days I wished I had held Richard more tightly. I would have spent every moment I could have with him had I known our days together would be cut short. That was not the way we lived, however. One of the things Richard loved about me was that I allowed him his autonomy, to let his life be his own. His devotion to the girls and me was never in question. I gave him the space to choose and so when he wanted to fly to New York for press interviews for his new book, even though he could have stayed and done satellite interviews from home, I went along with the plan.

"It's the final push," he said.

That was the thing. Richard was pushing and pushing hard. He was back to the early days of promoting and getting the word out. But he was exhausted. I asked him if he should go to the doctor because he was so tired but he told me he liked being tired. He had suffered insomnia most of his adult life, and I understood what he meant, knowing his sleep patterns well. We talked, as we'd been doing for months, about his boredom, not with writing, but with "the game." It wasn't fun to push sales. He was still talking about how he was ready for a big change. He talked about world peace. I truly felt fear grip me as I remember thinking, Oh Richard, please don't check out on me!

It's funny how we get these inklings and premonitions but we don't think they are real because they are muddled with all sorts of other thoughts. I couldn't really see the spiritual shifts that were happening before my eyes. Being human, we deny the possibility of death; otherwise, we would be afraid all the time. Still, I was oddly aware, as I'd been all fall, of a change happening in Richard, but I was unable to identify what it was. Now I know I was watching him getting ready for his departure *Home*.

He woke up the morning of December 12, walked into the kitchen, and said to Jazz, Kenna, and me, "I feel so good. I feel so happy."

He looked truly rested after sleeping for twelve hours, which was highly unusual for him. In fact, I never knew him to stay in bed for that length of time, ever. His back had been feeling much, much better lately. He was swimming regularly and feeling more himself. We went about the day, busy, busy as usual. I spent time with him that morning just getting a few things done. He helped me take some sweatshirts we'd just had printed to the office. Later that day, Richard did a couple of interviews that turned out to be very stressful, as there were technical difficulties with both and they had to be redone twice.

It was Richard's custom, when he had to be in New York, to take the first flight out so as not to lose the entire business day in flight. But we lived a good distance from the San Francisco Airport, and because he would have had to wake up at 3:00 A.M. to make his flight if he were home, he usually spent the night in a hotel out by the airfield. That last day, he called to say he'd decided to go into the city a little earlier than usual to beat the traffic and to relax a little.

After he died, Richard's overnight bag and briefcase were returned to me. It was a month before I could go through his briefcase. I pulled out the receipts from his hotel bill and dinner that charted the last night of his life. I carefully took everything out and set each bit of paper on the floor around me. I knew that he'd eaten a tofu and vegetable dish in the hotel restaurant and that he'd surfed three movies. "I loved my dinner," he had told me when we spoke over the phone before he went to bed that night, my last conversation with him.

The next morning, he took the shuttle to the airport and left a voice mail with his assistant, because at 5:00 A.M. it was too early in the morning to call me. He was exuberant as he boarded the plane. "I've never felt so caught up in my life," he told her. "My bills are paid. I feel refreshed." That man was going *Home*. God granted him an easy death.

Now, in my imagination, I was walking with him toward the passenger gate. I had to leave him there; I could go no farther. I think about looking into his ocean-blue eyes for the last time, and watching him as he disappeared down the departure ramp.

That is where my fantasy ends, and some anger creeps back in again. Many of the news reports mistakenly called his cause of death a heart attack, leaving a hurtful impression that one of the world's foremost authors on stress management could not manage his own.

They were wrong. Richard died of a blood clot that traveled from his leg to his lung. There was nothing wrong with his heart. It could have happened to anyone.

The environment that results in deep vein thrombosis happens over time, but Richard likely would not have noticed its symptoms. His back pain would have masked the leg pains and cramping he probably felt. He was used to being in pain and probably couldn't have differentiated the new from the old. Perhaps he elected not to stretch his long legs and walk around the aisles to get his circulation going or to drink enough fluids during the flight. Possibly he ignored any nausea and stomach upset he might have felt. It wouldn't be like him to complain; Richard wouldn't have wanted to trouble anyone.

Richard died on the descent into New York, probably around thirty thousand feet. I do believe that Richard knew on a spiritual level that he would be called back to God earlier than most. I hoped that His name was on Richard's lips when God took him from us.

Richard always said that Life is process, not a destination. And so, it is the same with Grief. Grieving is a process, not a destination. It is a full embrace of life and the circle of completion.

Leaving my family in the Pacific Northwest after a weekend celebrating my parents' fiftieth wedding anniversary, my daughters and I walked up to the airline-ticket agent. Looking up and over his glasses at our confirmation number on his computer screen, he said, "The three of you are not sitting together."

We looked at each other and I turned to the girls. "Are you two all right with that?"

They shrugged, "It's okay, it's a short flight, we're fine."

We checked our bags, and as we walked away, the agent called out to us. He said, "It's not a full flight; if you don't mind sitting in the exit row I can put you all together. You'll just have to be across the aisle."

I waved and said, "That was very kind of you. Thank you so much!"

We boarded the plane and a man took the seat next to mine. We struck up a short, friendly conversation. However, as the plane ascended, he pulled out his laptop and started to work.

I took my cue and quieted, keeping to myself. I pulled my own laptop out and wrote for a short while. On the descent, after he placed his laptop back in his briefcase, I attempted to converse again. "Is this a work day for you?" I asked.

He responded with a friendly smile and nodded. "Yes, I have a couple of meetings in San Francisco this afternoon. Sorry, didn't mean to be rude." I assured him that he wasn't rude at all. He asked, "What about you?"

I replied, "No, it's not a work day that way. I'm a writer." When he wondered if he might know any of my published work, I replied, "You might know of my late husband, Richard Carlson, author of *Don't' Sweat the Small Stuff*." An odd expression came over him as he looked away for a moment. I asked, "Have you read his books?"

He quietly said, "No, but I know of him. Did he die on a flight to JFK a while back?"

I wondered how he knew where Richard had been flying to and nodded. "Yes."

The man took a deep breath and said, "I was sitting directly behind your husband on that flight. I was one of the first to assist."

Meeting this gentleman and hearing, finally, the end of Richard's story, at a time when I was ready for it, completed another cycle of healing. Richard got on a plane and I never saw him in physical form again. Not in life, not in death. I intuited that this amazing coincidence was no accident, but a divine come-around. Another example that God wanted me to accept that it was Richard's time and it was in Divine Order.

The hand of the Divine revealed itself to me in another incident when I had to think of someone to identify Richard's body, someone who lived in New York. John Welshons was a man I'd only met once, but he was a dear friend of Richard's who would know how to find the hospital in Queens, New York. He agreed to be our liaison with the coroner's office. He called the morgue to make the appointment. The receptionist asked him to please come in at 2:00 P.M., Friday. John reached down for his daybook, opened it up, and for a moment was confused when he saw Richard's name already penciled in. Then John shook his head and laughed just before his tears came. He and Richard had scheduled a meeting for that exact time: 2:00 P.M. on Friday. They would meet after all, but not the way they had originally planned. Instead, they would meet according to divine plan.

The bathroom Richard and I shared was divided by a double shower, with his sink and cabinetry on one side of the transparent glass and mine on the other. The mirrors are wall to wall and installed by mastic, which is a tar-like adhesive that generally will only melt in a fire. The day before Richard died my mirror popped off the wall. It fell against the vanity lights and rested on its edge by one-eighth of an inch. I called a handyman out, and, as I was speaking with Richard on the phone during our final conversation, the man came and glued my mirror back down.

Richard and I were like mirror reflections of each other, meshing and moving together; that was the beauty of our life. But during the last months when I knew something was shifting but didn't know what, heaviness nagged at me, like I was weighted down. Now I saw that unease was reflected by my mirror becoming unglued and by Richard's onerous back pain. As I put these isolated coincidences together – the gentleman on the airplane, John's daybook, and the mirror – against the progression of his last months, I finally understood what I had gone over in my mind hundreds of times. I wasn't meant to intervene. The divine makes itself known. It is what it is.

It is, as it was meant to be.

December 13, 2007

The publisher called to tell me they were pushing ahead the publication date for *An Hour to Live, an Hour to Love*, which was already in its third printing. Copies of the book would arrive in the stores today, in fact. Today was also the first anniversary of Richard's death.

The past month felt like a whirlwind. How could life hold any more? I asked myself. It was ironic to me that during that long year after Richard died, I seemingly lived so fully. What was that?

That night the girls and I were holding a candle lighting at our home to honor Richard and the light he still carried in the world. It was another coincidence that Richard passed on Saint Lucia Day. She is the Swedish Saint of Love and Kindness and is also regarded as an inspiration to writers. Saint Lucia brought the light into the darkness of the Scandinavian winter to offer hope and encouragement during that harsh season.

We were expecting one hundred guests here and planned to light candles and float them in the pool in celebration of Saint Lucia, the roots of our family, and our beloved Richard. Jazz, Kenna, and I decorated the tree with family photographs, *Don't Sweat the Small Stuff* treasury books, messages in glass ornaments, hearts, and white lights. I noticed feeling a lightness that day that I knew would carry me through the small hours. The girls were teasing each other as they hung the lights.

The house had candles everywhere. I shut my eyes for a moment, and then opened them wide. It had never looked more magical.

21.

CAPACITY FOR LOVE

It was Sunday morning and everyone was laughing and in a good mood, hanging out in the kitchen, each doing something different. Kenna sat at the counter eating a toast and egg sandwich Richard had prepared for her, and Jazz bounced in and asked him to make one for her, too. Looking every bit the short-order cook, he served me my coffee just as I liked it, with soy milk all whipped at the top. Jazz laughed and said, "Dad, there aren't any men like you!"

Both girls said aloud, "Mom, you are so lucky. You are treated like a queen."

I laughed and looked over at him in praise. "I know. I'm so screwed if something happens to your dad." Richard was smiling at being lovingly appreciated by his three girls.

One and a half years later, the camera rolled as I sat in a chair opposite the host of a television news program. I was doing more publicity for *An Hour to Live, an Hour to Love* and the host and I were talking about Richard's authenticity and life. Then the host turned to me and asked a question, in its way almost as big for me as the big question Richard had just answered in that book. "It's been a year now; are you dating? What's that like and how could you possibly meet men with the standards set by Richard Carlson? How do you know, Kris, you can love deeply again?"

It was hard for me to answer this question in the same breath as I spoke about my marriage and love for Richard. I am not looking for a replacement. There is no replacing Richard, who loved me so completely and who made me feel so safe. I knew that it was going to take a man with self-possession to live in the shadow of Richard's legacy and who could embrace life in a bigger way than in accordance with traditional standards. My needs were quite different now than they were when I was younger.

After eleven months of grief, I was deeply feeling the need for male companionship again, but I was not at all ready to embrace being in the singles world. During a warm July evening my girlfriend and I met her good friend Randy for some wine and appetizers. She felt there was something so similar about the two of us in the way we connect with her that she hoped we would spawn a friendship that might help me through this phase of loneliness. Three months later, in October, I worked up my nerve and called him to see if he wanted to enjoy a glass of wine.

As I was getting ready, I felt both nervous and excited. I selected my clothes carefully – skinny jeans and a pretty printed shirt that was just a little bit sheer and sexy. I wore boots with stiletto heels and a long black suede jacket. My hair was down and I did my face with light evening makeup. It was a treat getting ready to go out with a man, and it had been years since I had been on a date like this. After discussing where to meet and declining a few places that Richard and I had frequented together, we settled on dinner at a very nice Italian restaurant. I walked in and Randy was sitting in front at the bar. I noticed again as I had last summer how attractive he was. He turned his head slightly and saw me. I sensed his approval as we greeted one another. Our conversation was easy. He listened attentively and contributed intelligent comments on all kinds of topics. I asked him, "What happened in your marriage?"

He replied as he lifted his wineglass to his lips, "That's second date conversation. I don't want to get into that right away."

I laughed and said, "Fair enough," as we hadn't had any shortage of things to say to each other.

It felt comfortable with this man. He felt familiar to me in the way people do when I am deeply connected to them. He was passionate about great food and wine, and we ordered like a king and a queen. He had the pork chop and I had salmon and we shared a salad and a bottle of

Rombauer zin. We discovered that we both loved banana everything, so we ordered a baked banana served oozing with hot fudge and real whipped cream.

For a moment I wished I had asked someone what "the rules" were in dating etiquette now, as I wasn't sure if I should offer to pay my half of the check. But he reached for the bill with a firm gesture that told me there was no question that he was paying. He drove me to my car in the parking structure and I could have easily thanked him and just gotten out; instead, I leaned over and put my head back to kiss him goodnight. I was curious if we had chemistry. He was very respectful and kept it gentle and not at all demanding. We kissed for several minutes, and I felt a melting kind of passion stir in me, like I was a schoolgirl. When I broke away, we shared a moment of laughter as we said it totally felt like a high school moment. As I drove away, my thoughts surprised me. I pondered the idea that I was genuinely physically attracted to Randy. He had dark good looks, an athletic body, and a quick, tender smile. He also had a youthful quality that I adored in Richard. I could see the young boy still inside the man; somehow, there are men who keep that boyish innocence, which is so desirable.

Talk about breaking the ice. I couldn't have felt more comfortable during a first real date. I woke with a smile, and I knew I probably shouldn't, but I called him the next day to thank him and tell him I had a wonderful evening and I really hoped we would go out again. He said, "It's great that you called. I love how you just say and do what you want to and don't overthink it."

Well, I thought to myself, I don't know how to play the game and have no desire to learn the rules. I just want to be me. I was leaving for Italy in a few days for The Path of Love spiritual workshop and we agreed to get together when I returned.

Our connection grew very quickly and perhaps, for him, it was too fast. He told me, "You are like a freight train of energy, and I am not sure how I jumped on so fast." I knew what he was talking about because during this period I, too, was experiencing a transformation, as the random pieces of my life seemed to connect along a continuum, a high wire electrified and vibrating with new life. It didn't seem to matter where I was or with whom; I even connected with people wherever I found myself with this grief-awakened intensity. As I came out into the world, open and raw, it allowed anyone I was in contact with the permission to meet me in that place. People this year showed me in so many new ways that they want love and connection more than anything else in the world.

Randy gave me plenty of space to grieve. He listened for endless hours with unwavering patience; he didn't mind that I needed to share my stories about my life with Richard. He didn't feel competitive, knowing that he was bringing something totally different to me during a very unique time.

Randy would cook for me – most of our time was spent that way. He would take care of me with the same care he took in preparing our meal. They were simple meals, beautifully presented: sea bass and ahi tuna with arugula salad adorned with fennel and mandarin oranges. Omelets or banana chocolate chip pancakes in the morning when I woke to the smell of bacon frying. His cooking was so tactile: He rubbed his ahi steaks with olive oil and then seared them. He would drizzle butter lettuce with lemon and sea salt, and use his fingers to toss everything together. He made the most astounding chocolate peanut butter truffles! I would sit on his kitchen counter and sip champagne and watch him prepare a meal. Later, Randy would hold me when lovemaking would trigger an unrelenting wave of surrender and grief as my body lay in his arms, racked by sobs. He knew how much it hurt, and remained present. It had to be difficult for him, but he stayed when many men would not have known how to hold such pain and sorrow. He gave to me, and I fell in love.

Randy had healed a lot himself, following the pain of his divorce years before, and a deep connection grew between us. I felt like this was a man who knew loss and could hold the space for me that I needed in my second year of grief. He was a rock to grab on to as a storm would blow in, not only in grief, but also in my life that held many new challenges and transitions. He thought his role was going to be to see me through to my next relationship. I see it differently. He has been there to hold my head as I find my way back to my true Self.

I realize that my needs as a woman and a widow are so different now. What I need is a man who will take care of me and be my safe place to land – funny, as that is very much like the role I played for Richard. The one thing that is the same is that I need to know I am loved as thoroughly as I loved Richard, and he me. This is the only way for me to love. I don't know what the future holds, but I remain ever present in the moment. I am grateful to Randy for the opportunity to share love again and to see proof of my own ever-expanding capacity for love.

After we had been dating for a month, I told Jazz that I was "dating" Randy. She was most concerned that he wasn't some random guy I had picked up somewhere. (As if I was into hookups!). She was happy when I explained that Sharon had introduced us. Jazz was very supportive and didn't want me to be lonely. When I told Kenna, she had a totally different reaction. "How could you do that to Daddy?" she cried. I completely understood why my news was difficult for her. She still had two years left to live at home with me, and she had heard stories where mothers had remarried or moved in with men within a year of a separation or death.

I assured Kenna that she was my number one priority and Randy had no interest in disrupting the balance of our home. I told her I wished I were more like a nun, but I was not. I was a woman in the prime of midlife, and I would wither up like a rose without water if I didn't have some male companionship. I said, "There is never going to be any person who will take Daddy's place in my heart, but my heart is big enough to share more love. Daddy would want me to feel love again."

It was yet another adjustment, but we all took it very slowly, and eventually Kenna embraced a new change and transition and accepted that I was her "single" mom.

My relationship with Randy has continued to soften the edge of grief and made it bearable as I continue on my journey with a man I trusted to hold my heart in his hands.

I turn back to the TV interviewer. I look straight into her eyes; there is no need to look away or into my lap where my hands are neatly folded. Richard taught me well. I could handle this question and all the others that might come my way, large and small. *It's not what you say; it's how it feels inside when you say it.*

"How do I know that I am going to love deeply again?" I repeat. "It's like having a first child. You feel that you can't possibly love a second child that much. And then, when the second child arrives, you love it as much as you love the first one. We have an infinite capacity for love. We love people differently because in relationships we reveal to each other different aspects of who we are. We can love people differently but still love them deeply, because that's what love is."

The interview over, I got up, removed the tiny wireless microphone, and shook the host's hand.

As I gathered my things, I asked myself a follow-up question. I thought about Richard and the depth of the love we shared for twenty-five years. "Who will ever love me like that again?" I asked.

I know the answer. Somewhere inside, I believe I was meant to love myself the way Richard loved me – with unconditional acceptance. There were still nights when I lay awake in our bed, touching our India coverlet, and thought that maybe it is enough to be loved like that once in a lifetime. And yet the idea that I might live the rest of my life alone remains one of my greatest fears.

What I am continuing to discover is that I am never alone, because I have me.

Four

RELEASE & RECEIVE

... Rebirth a New Life

22.

ON THE WINGS OF LOVE

August 2009

In the beginning I thought I would be in deep grief forever. I thought surely as deeply as I loved Richard, I would be lost in sorrow. Now, looking back, I clearly have learned differently. I will miss Richard for the rest of my life, and the longing will remind me to stay awake and present. Love is what has carried me into my suffering. Love is what has carried me out of it as well. Suffering opened me and now love moves me forward.

I've heard it said that red-tailed hawks mate for life. We live in a valley where the sun penetrates the trees in great slanting sheets of light and turns the air iridescent. When I look up I often see one hawk flying solo, and she has given me much hope. She just soars, and I say to myself, "I can do that! I can fly solo, too, if I am meant to." I can do that now. I am more me than I ever have been. I find it ironic that in the absence of my great love I have learned the lessons of living and loving presently. I am a testament to Richard's work on earth because I received all the tools he had to teach, and now I live them. I can say with a smile that I live "The Big Stuff," and it really is true: *You can feel good again. You can be happy no matter what.*

Everything is further and further away from that time when I thought my life would collapse. I have turned my personal tragedy into something else. It was a beautiful opportunity for me to spend that first year in transparent reflection. It was a gift to be able to go through our life remembering the joyous times and making peace with those things I might do differently in a second time around – *if only.*

Accept life as it is Now

Surrender, Trust, Accept, and RECEIVE a new life. These words gave me a path through loss and into a new life. Every time I faced something I just told myself: "Surrender to life," trusting in life and love to lead the way, and accept life as it is now. While we learned that mantra long ago, Richard wrote about that, too, and now I see how this mantra penetrated our life. We lived it thoughtfully and consciously aware, but I didn't realize how close we really did live to all of what he wrote until I had to live it in loss. It became clear to me that Richard created the template for living.

My two and a half years of healing have left me feeling clear and happy. I think about how I learned I can live with grief, how loss can transform, and about the adventure I am living now. After Richard died I could see myself drowning and dying, and I could see myself living and grieving. Somehow, I understood that grieving could be one of the most important and replenishing tasks of my life, and that if I followed my intuition and committed to staying present in this moment, I could heal. The loss of my dearest friend and life partner knocked me down in a big way, but I not only got back up, I got back up to live life more fully awake. I got back up because of him. Richard's death has made me more alive.

Miracles happen all around us if we are open to seeing and receiving them. I continue to believe in the healing power of coincidences and synchronicity just as I did in those first days after Richard passed. I do believe there is a thin veil that shows us that God, light, and love are always present.

I have experienced Richard's presence several times this past summer. In a recent dream Richard and I are flying in a Land Cruiser. He was steering from outside the car and I was in the backseat. When I considered the dream, I understood that I am at last ready to let go, to get into the driver's seat and take control of the wheel. He is still present and still very much a part of me as I move through my life, but I am taking control of the car and my way through life.

Then, just two days after my birthday, I was in line at Starbucks. I was standing in the pickup line with my friends while they waited for their coffee. I bought a banana nut muffin and was regretting that I had not ordered a latte. I thought of Richard and how surprised he would be that I was cutting back, and even considering giving up coffee. He brought me coffee every morning as we watched the sun rise on a new day together. He was the person who introduced me to coffee while we were in college and fell in love. One moment later, someone from behind the pickup counter called out, "Richard!" A man stepped forward to retrieve his coffee, turned around, and, holding two cups in his hands, said to me: "Hey, they gave me two by mistake, would you like one?" I smiled as he handed me a large cup of java with the word "Richard" pencil-scrawled on the lid. Smiling to myself, I thought, That's no mistake. That's my Richard.

These are the moments that push back my sorrow. They remind me that love is eternal and formless. I can, and will always, meet Richard in my own heart.

I recently came in from a night out with my girlfriends, washed my face, brushed my teeth, and climbed into bed. It was a rare night because when I woke up in the morning, I realized I had actually slept all the way through. This was the first night I could remember doing that in all the time since Richard passed. I woke up smiling, and I woke up on *his* side of the bed.

Through our years together I always took the right side. As I lay in bed I felt the impression of his body still in our mattress. That night I slipped onto his side again, this time with the intention that comes from a quiet heart, and I slept like a baby for the second time in over two years. I realized I was no longer waiting for him to slip into bed beside me. I had come full circle into "acceptance."

It's hard to imagine the places we go. All we can be sure of is that life will change again and again, and yet again. I sleep on the left side of the bed now every night and when I wake up, most mornings, I wake in joy. I am happy for no other reason except that I am alive and breathing. I wonder, "What's today going to bring?" I don't worry. I don't plan out too far. I'm allowing every day to unfold. Life will show me what's next. That takes a lot of the pressure off – a welcome change from trying to hold life and control it. That's complete surrender.

I never thought I would feel this good again.

Life is all about beginnings and endings. Richard's ashes are still on the top shelf of his closet, the closet we now share, and where his baseball cap winks at me whenever I glance up. Most people take care of distributing the blessed remains of their departed quickly; for me, I hadn't found the right time. I wanted that last "letting go" to hold the meaning it was supposed to have. I waited for a special date, and partly I waited for my girls to come to full acceptance. I wanted them to embrace the fullness of what happened from the place of strength they feel *now*. And the time has come. At Sea Ranch there is a bench near the end of the cliff that looks out to the ocean. This is where Richard gave me *An Hour to Live, an Hour to Love*. We often sat on this bench together as the day closed and the sun slipped into the fuchsia sea. It is here I feel Richard would have wanted his ashes to be spread, in this sacred setting and intimate, family place. We are planning to do that on Richard's birthday this year as our gift to him and to ourselves.

But there is a beginning in this ending, too. On August 10, 2009, at 4:19 A.M. my daughter Jasmine gave birth to Caden Richard. I sat in the delivery room holding one of Jazz's feet, Kenna standing at her shoulder, and her future husband, Brennan, holding her other foot until that moment and that final push when Caden's head crowned and he torpedoed into his father's arms. I watched the love shining brightly in the eyes of this new family, while inside I shook as the gentle tremor of memory rippled through me. In my mind's eye, it was Jasmine who was entering the world. I saw Richard's face beside me, so full of happiness and eager anticipation, I felt the flood of all our yesterdays, just as Kenna, Jasmine, Brennan, and Caden are beginning all of their tomorrows. Now there is a new baby. He brings a piece of Richard back to us, and to this earth, to carry on.

In a vision of where I am today, as I have come through the valley floor, up the mountain and to the summit, I stand on the edge of a ridge ready to jump – thirty thousand feet. My arms held out and legs in spread-eagle, I embrace all that I am: I am here now! I am vibrant and alive! I stand at the edge, ready to soar like the red-tailed hawk that lives in my valley. I know with certainty that Richard's love will always be my parachute, and that I will ride on the wings of his love as he brings me *Home*.

ABOUT THE AUTHOR

Kristine Carlson is the #1 *New York Times Bestselling Author* of *The Don't Sweat the Small Stuff* series co-authored with her late husband Dr Richard Carlson.

Her memoir, *Heartbroken Open* is the intimate story of her love and life with Richard and the life-changing, life-affirming rediscovery that happened following his unexpected death.

Eleven years after its original release, *Heartbroken Open* became a biopic Lifetime Television movie starring the iconic actress, Heather Locklear, titled, *Don't Sweat the Small Stuff: The Kristine Carlson Story.*

With over 30 million books in print, Kristine's expertise has been featured on *The Today Show*, *The View*, and *The Oprah Winfrey Show*.

Kristine has an unwavering life mission to share how it's possible to turn pain into purpose and rediscover laughter, love, and happiness after a major life change. Her story is a true gift and a necessary touchpoint for anyone who has experienced great loss.

To learn more about Kristine Carlson, visit
kristinecarlson.com